# INLAND BIRDS OF
# SAUDI ARABIA

# INLAND BIRDS OF SAUDI ARABIA

*Jill Silsby*

IMMEL
Publishing

*Inland Birds of Saudi Arabia*
Designed and produced by Cigale Limited
34 Stansfield Road, London SW9
for IMMEL Publishing
First published 1980

© 1980 Jill Silsby
ISBN 0 907151 00 0

Phototypeset in Bembo by Filmtype Services Limited
Scarborough, Yorkshire, England
Printed and bound in Japan by
Dai Nippon Printing Co, Tokyo

*Design & art direction:* Cigale Limited
*Art assistant:* Karen Popham
*House editor:* Janet MacLennan
*Ornithological adviser:* Andrew Gosler BSc, MBOU

Page 1: *European Bee-eater,* Merops apiaster, *is
one of the most strikingly coloured birds of the
desert. This species may frequently be seen perching
on telegraph wires in desert areas where natural
perches are scarce.*

Pages 2 and 3: *Black-tailed Scrub Warbler,*
Scotocerca inquieta, *is a restless little bird that
may be difficult to find in the dense acacia scrub that
it frequents. This bird is usually found by accident
as it normally skulks in undergrowth, but becomes
highly agitated when alarmed.*

# Contents

# Foreword

**BUCKINGHAM PALACE.**

I am addicted to books about birds anyway but when I travel abroad, which happens from time to time, I find the appropriate bird books invaluable. Sadly there are many parts of the world which have not had the advantage of the British mania for identifying, collecting, classifying, and categorising 'all creatures great and small'. This book fills a big gap and I am sure it will be welcomed by everyone interested in birds and particularly by those who find themselves working in or visiting the Arabian peninsula.

1980

# Preface

The aim of this book is to describe and illustrate with photographs as many of the birds present in the Arabian peninsula as possible. Since a book of this nature must be limited by considerations of size I decided to exclude all birds (with the exception of moorhens and coots) that swim, thus eliminating gulls, grebes, ducks, cormorants and phalaropes and so on.

Coverage of Arabian birds has tended to be somewhat meagre. This book will, I hope, put Arabia south of Jordan and Iraq on the *avi fauna* map again. Also, there are big glossy books dealing rather generally with birds from a wide area and illustrated by superb photographs and there are small more detailed Field Guides giving a lot of information and illustrated by small paintings or drawings. I hope in this book to combine some of the advantages of both.

Bird photography, under the best conditions, is difficult and time-consuming. Under a hot Arabian sun and with no possibility of setting up a hide or of carrying a tripod around, it can, at times, prove almost impossible. There are, therefore, a few birds I have been completely unable to get on the camera and several more illustrated with less than perfect photographs. On the whole I have, I think, been incredibly lucky.

At this point I think I should say that in a book of this nature it is impossible to be completely free from error and I certainly do not claim to be infallible. Also, on a few occasions I have photographed birds that neither I nor consulted experts have been able to identify. In most cases these have been omitted from the text though perhaps in a future edition they will have been identified and can then be included.

It will become obvious that the bulk of the observations have been made in central Arabia – I was resident in Riyadh from October 1977 to May 1980. However, prior to and during that period, visits were made to Abu Dhabi, Dubai and Sharjah and several short trips to Taif, Jeddah, Dhahran, Asir, Oman and Bahrain. For records of birds mentioned in the text in areas that I have not visited and of birds that I have not personally observed I am indebted to keen and knowledgeable bird-watching friends – Arthur Stagg (northwest), Tom Walcot (Hejaz and Asir), Tim Murphy and Mike Jennings (centre and elsewhere). To these four, to Alan Whitehead for processing my films during the last frantic days, and to Phil Hollom and Richard Porter for such valuable help with identification I would like to express my appreciation and very sincere thanks.

I am also greatly indebted to David Dinnell, Betty Vincett, Mike Jennings, Heather Ross and Frank Naylor for letting me use some of their beautiful photographs. Photographs provided by each are marked accordingly. I would like, also, to express my warm appreciation of the encouragement I received from Dr Abdul Aziz H Al Sowayyegh and his predecessor H E Dr Fouad Al Farsy at the Ministry of Information. Finally, and most importantly, I wish to thank my husband Ronnie for his endless patience and ever-growing enthusiasm. He has been chauffeur, porter, habitat photographer, map-maker and general morale-booster. Without him this book would never have been completed nor even, probably, begun.

*Jill Silsby,* JUNE 1980

# Introduction

Mention the word 'Arabia' and two completely different pictures spring to mind. Most visitors to the Peninsula see the large modern cities with their magnificent buildings, paved roads and burgeoning industry. A lucky few find time to get out of the towns and into the countryside where an ever decreasing number of people prefer to lead the traditional nomadic life. In both these dramatically different environments few people visualise birdlife when the word 'Arabia' is mentioned. Let us, therefore, take a look at Arabia and see how and where birds fit into the picture.

The Arabian peninsula, which is broadly rectangular in shape, is interposed between the African and Asian land masses, being separated from the former by the Red Sea and from the latter by the Arabian Gulf. The southern edge is bordered by the Indian Ocean while in the north it is connected to the remainder of the Middle East through Jordan and Iraq. It lies roughly in the middle of the broad band of desert and semi-desert extending from the Western Sahara to the Gobi and its climate, as a result, is (on the whole) arid with summer temperatures reaching 50°C and an annual rainfall seldom exceeding about ten centimetres. Much of the peninsula is occupied by the Kingdom of Saudi Arabia; the other countries are concentrated round the southwestern, southern, southeastern and eastern coasts.

Although most of the peninsula can broadly be described as desert, the geography and topography of the region have produced considerable variation. The land is tilted from west to east, with a mountain chain (exhibiting much former volcanic activity) all the way down the Red Sea coast and the land sloping gradually down from this to the Arabian Gulf in the east. The southern part of this mountain chain reaches 3000 to 3500 metres and in this area the rainfall is relatively plentiful,

resulting in abundant vegetation. In ancient times the area was known as 'Arabia Felix'; today part of it lies in North Yemen and the rest forms the southwestern province of Saudi Arabia – Asir. The southern coast also receives some rain, particularly where – in eastern Oman – the other significant mountain range rises to around 3000 metres. The central and eastern parts of the peninsula are composed almost entirely of sedimentary rocks and, here and there, the generally downward trend from west to east is interrupted by an upward step, produced by fracture of the strata. At these points underground water following the strata may be forced to the surface, leading to strips of vegetation (and sometimes cultivation) below the step. The largest of these steps is the Tuwaiq Escarpment which traverses much of the peninsula on a generally north to south axis and which changes direction immediately west of Riyadh to run southwest rather than southeast, with fairly complex faulting. In past eras, when rainfall was more plentiful, water carved out ravines or wadis, usually rising on the eastern slopes of these escarpments and flowing in a generally easterly or southeasterly direction. Today these wadis are dry except immediately after heavy rain, but in their lower reaches they can provide access to underground water for irrigation, allowing the establishment of palm groves and larger cultivated areas. Riyadh lies on one of the larger of these wadis (Wadi Hanifah) and, in fact, the name Riyadh means 'garden' in Arabic.

The erosion of the sedimentary rocks has produced sand and stones, the former accumulating mainly in hollows, large and small. There is one large sand desert in the north of the country (the Nafud) and an even larger one extending right across the peninsula in the south, representing the largest unbroken sand desert in the world – the Rubh al Khali or Empty

Quarter. The broadly north/south 'grain' of the country results in narrower belts of sand with this general orientation; the largest of these (Ad Dhana) connects the Nafud to the Empty Quarter. Most of the sand belts are, however, considerably shorter and narrower than this and between sand belts the central and eastern regions consist largely of stone desert, often almost bare of vegetation except where interrupted by wadis or the fault escarpments.

One thing that surprises most newcomers to the desert is its natural beauty. The sand desert is the most striking with its reddish dunes, sculptured by the wind and stretching endlessly to the horizon. Even the relatively featureless stone desert has a beauty of its own, probably best appreciated when seen at night under a full moon. The fantastic shapes etched by wind and sand in the high cliffs of the escarpments seem to change both form and colour as the sun changes elevation and moves across the sky. Into all this the Bedouin camp, with its long, low dark brown camel or goat-hair tents, seems to fit perfectly, as do the flocks of sheep and goats which, together with camels and donkeys, are so typical of the country-side, where, in contrast to city life, the pace is more leisurely.

Perhaps the most astonishing thing in such seemingly inhospitable surroundings is the abundance of life almost everywhere. Acacia thorn and other perennial plants are able to survive the most arid conditions, while the seeds of annuals can lie dormant for years before carpeting the desert with flowers after heavy rain. Numerous insect species have similarly adapted themselves, as have certain smaller mammals and reptiles. This means that everything needed to sustain the life of birds (shade, seeds, insects and even occasional water) is present in all but the most arid parts of the desert. While the largest bird populations are to be found in the

SYRIA

IRAN

IRAQ

JORDAN

Jawf

Tabuk

*NAFUD*

Hail

KUWAIT

EASTERN PROVINCE

*ARABIAN GULF*

Buraydah

QASIM

Dammam

BAHRAIN

QATAR

Hofuf

Doha

Sharjah

Dubai

Fujairah

Medina

RIYADH

Abu Dhabi

U.A.E.

Yanbu

*Jebel Akhdar*

Muscat

HEJAZ

*Jebel Tuwaiq*

OMAN

Jeddah

**Mecca**

Taif

*RED SEA*

HEJAZ

ASIR

R U B   A L   K H A L I

Abha

Najran

Jizan

NORTH YEMEN

SOUTH YEMEN

Salalah

San'a

*ARABIAN SEA*

Mukalla

Aden

N

SAND DESERT

0–1000m

OVER 1000m

ESCARPMENT

0km          500

DAHNA

N E J D

wadis and other vegetated areas, around villages or near water, some species are to be found almost everywhere if one looks hard enough.

Arabia holds a unique position as far as bird-life is concerned. It can be regarded as a four-way bridge connecting north to south and east to west. Thus birds usually recognised as African are present in the southwest, Oriental birds in the southeast and European birds in the northwest. Further, the peninsula lies on two distinct migratory routes, one from western Europe via the Mediterranean and down the Red Sea coast to East Africa and the other a broad one from eastern Europe via the Tigris and Euphrates valley to the head of the Arabian Gulf and down through the centre of the peninsula on a direct route to Ethiopia and the rest of Africa. A side-shoot of this route follows the Gulf making a less direct journey to the same destination. Areas of permanent water provide welcome 'stop-overs' for migrating birds and they will take the opportunity to rest and feed before taking off again to complete their journeys. They remain for varying lengths of time; some will be off after just a couple of days, others may stay a few weeks; in a few cases birds travelling from the north to winter in Africa decide to call a halt in Arabia – thus there are several species present as winter visitors. In one or two cases the same happens in reverse to provide a few summer visitors as well. To this feast of bird-life can be added those birds that are particular to the Middle-East and a few that are peculiar to the peninsula alone.

One of the most beautiful and spectacular areas within the peninsula is undoubtedly that part of Asir around Abha. Most of the mountain tops are wild and craggy, others have their outlines softened by juniper. Here can be found the Lammergeier and Griffon Vultures together with the eagles and buzzards. Seated on rocks at the edge of Jebel Soodah, where the cliffs fall steeply several thousand feet to the valley below, these birds can be observed, from above, gliding on the

*Palm groves at Diraiyah.*

## Desert habitat types

*The desert consists of many types. Each has its own geography, and thus its own birds.*

Top left: *Stoney desert. The picture shows a typical flat desert plain with little vegetation of sufficient height for birds to use.*

Centre left: *A slight improvement on the stoney desert is the scrub desert. The acacia trees provide a more suitable habitat for birds.*

Bottom left: *A Bedouin camp in the scrub desert. Small camps like this may provide temporary feeding sites for birds.*

Centre: *Tuwaiq escarpment. Although these tall cliffs are a harsh environment, to many birds of prey they offer attractive nesting sites. Here they can raise their young high out of the reach of predators.*
Middle right: *Sand dune desert. Formed by the wind depositing sand around a solid nucleus, this habitat offers no vegetation for birds to feed on.*
Bottom: *Wadi above Towqi. Wadis provide the most valuable habitat for birds in the desert. Water, shade, food and nesting sites abound, and many passage migrants may be found in them.*

thermals of air and this is a truly wonderful sight. In the deep, well-wooded wadis (where every possible space is terraced and cultivated, each terrace being bordered with red sorrel or lavender) there is an abundance of small birds – linnets, sunbirds, White-Eyes, Redstarts – and their songs fill

possessing the grandeur and size of Asir, nor of the mountains of Oman and UAE, are beautiful in their own way. The area around Al Kharj, 77 kilometres south of Riyadh is fertile and well-cultivated. There are dairies, farms and large palm groves and here the birds that are found in the wadis

Below: *Terraced cultivation in Asir provides a valuable habitat for birds.*

Right: *The mountains of Asir provide good country for raptors.*

the air. In the less hospitable areas, where the rocks are bare, with only sporadic vegetation there are still birds to be found – wheatears, larks, babblers and Tristram's Grackle with its haunting song. This whole area is a bird-watcher's paradise.

In Hejaz there are well-vegetated wadis running from the high ground down to the coast and in these inlets, many of which are very beautiful, a wide variety of unusual birds can be found – Hamerkop, Glossy Ibis, Spoonbill, storks and the Demoiselle Crane. Grey Hornbills, Arabian Woodpeckers and Ruppell's Weavers are also present here as well as higher up in the Asir.

In the main body of the peninsula there are smaller areas that, while not

nearer Riyadh are present in much larger numbers. About 300 kilometres southwest of Al Kharj lies Layla with its deep lakes almost on the edge of the Rub al Khali. This is a fascinating area and a very popular one for weekend expeditions and picnics. Although the lakes are too deep to attract many waders, there are aquatic birds such as grebes and several species of duck as well as the ubiquitous coot and moorhen. In the scrub between the lakes bird life is prolific.

Around Riyadh itself there are many small oases of peace and beauty. To enter a palm grove in the Wadis Hanifah, Awsat or Amariyah, for instance, is to experience a relief that almost defies expression. The immediate drop in temperature, the

16

greenness to rest the eyes and the carefully rationed water on the ground provide a haven, not only for the human visitor, but for a great variety of birds as well. Namaqua Doves, Black Bush Robins, Blackstarts and some of the warblers can be found at all times of the year. Cuckoos, Orioles and Wrynecks take refuge during migration and Rufous Bush Chats, Redstarts, White-Throated Robins and many species of warbler are happily present for much longer periods.

Out in the desert itself, particularly scrub desert, areas with acacia and at the base of escarpments, there are still birds around – larks, wheatears, Cream-Coloured Coursers, partridge, Trumpeter Finches, House Buntings and ravens. A Blue Rock Thrush may sit on an old ruined building or a Stone Curlew may get up from the shelter of a low shrub almost at the walker's feet. From September to March Steppe Eagles can frequently be seen soaring overhead and at all times of the year there will be the occasional Hoopoe and Egyptian Vulture.

There are one or two areas, particularly round Mansouriyah, where the wadis are kept permanently full of water from sewage plants. During migration these areas are much in demand by a great variety of waders as well as bee-eaters and shrikes. A number of waders such as Little Stints, Green Sandpipers, Ruffs and Reeves appear to be settling in these areas as they can be found at all times of the year. Herons, egrets, Marsh Harriers and kestrels also find these areas very suitable habitats and visits by bird-watchers can be very rewarding indeed.

Finally, the peninsula is surrounded on three sides by the sea and along the entire coast-line there are, of course, an enormous variety of gulls, terns and waders of all description. The following pages will, I hope, show that the geographical and topographical variety of the peninsula is echoed by the wide variation of its birdlife.

*Sunset at Layla Lakes. Water in quantity forms an important habitat itself.*

19

# Topography of a Bird

## Arrangement of birds in this book

Since, in many cases, Orders of birds are represented in Arabia by just one specie, it has been found less cumbersome to arrange this book not in the generally accepted order, but into fourteen chapters. Thus among *Birds of sombre plumage*, for instance, will be found members of several Orders. Within each chapter, related birds are to be found beside each other and a line separates one Order from the next.

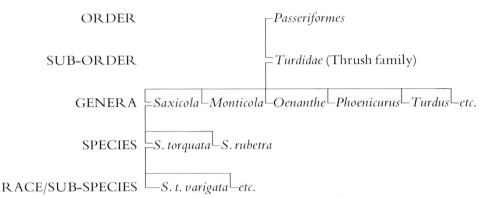

ORDER — *Passeriformes*

SUB-ORDER — *Turdidae* (Thrush family)

GENERA — *Saxicola* — *Monticola* — *Oenanthe* — *Phoenicurus* — *Turdus* — etc.

SPECIES — *S. torquata* — *S. rubetra*

RACE/SUB-SPECIES — *S. t. varigata* — etc.

## Principal features of a bird

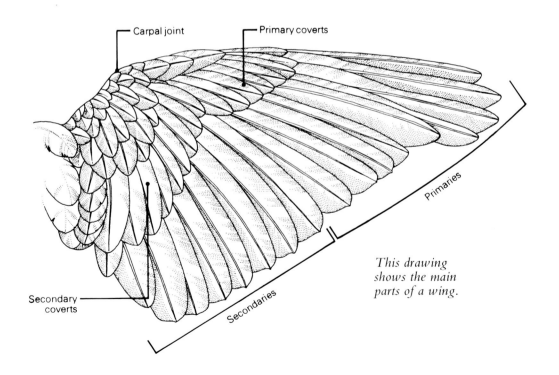

Carpal joint

Primary coverts

Primaries

Secondaries

Secondary coverts

*This drawing shows the main parts of a wing.*

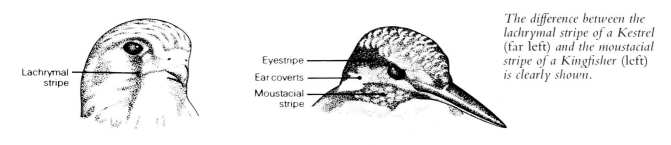

Lachrymal
stripe

Eyestripe

Ear coverts

Moustacial
stripe

*The difference between the
lachrymal stripe of a Kestrel
(far left) and the moustacial
stripe of a Kingfisher (left)
is clearly shown.*

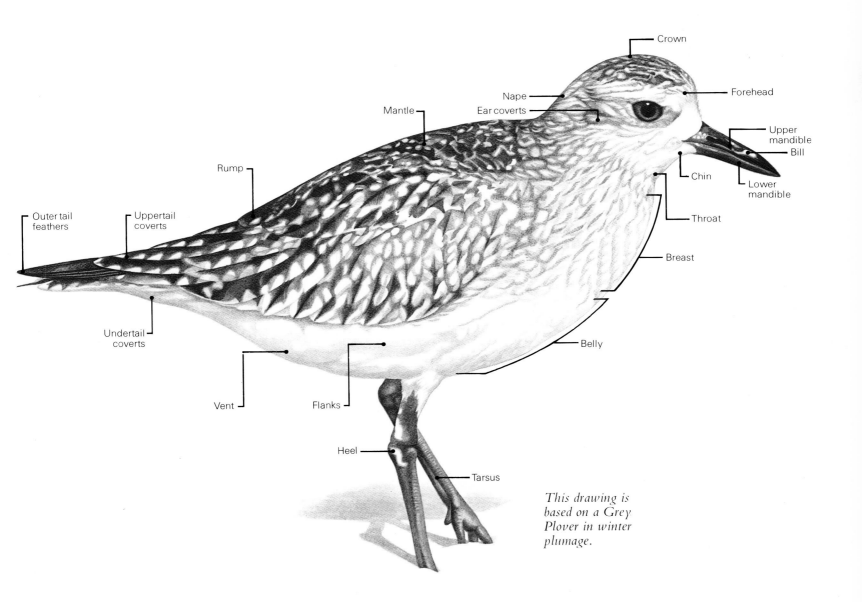

Crown

Forehead

Nape

Mantle

Ear coverts

Upper
mandible

Bill

Rump

Chin

Lower
mandible

Throat

Outer tail
feathers

Uppertail
coverts

Breast

Undertail
coverts

Belly

Vent

Flanks

Heel

Tarsus

*This drawing is
based on a Grey
Plover in winter
plumage.*

All the birds in this chapter are flesh-eaters, some preferring to kill their own prey and others being content with the carcasses of dead animals. Among them are some of the most majestic and awe-inspiring birds seen on Earth.

Below: *The unmistakable pattern of an Egyptian Vulture.*

# Vultures

These large to very large birds are scruffy and ungainly on the ground but majestic and, in some cases, beautiful in flight. Their long, wide wings enable them to soar at great heights from where they scan the ground below for a dead camel or goat and, at the same time, search the sky around for signs of other vultures gliding down towards a carcass, perhaps many miles away. Sexes are alike both in size and plumage. Immatures are of generally sombre plumage, lacking the distinguishing features of the adult.

Above: *At rest, this Egyptian Vulture shows the value of artificial perches and gives an indication of its relatively small size.*

## EGYPTIAN VULTURE
*Neophron percnopterus*
23–26 inches (58–66cm)
Wingspan 60–72 inches

*Identification:* The Egyptian Vulture is the smallest of the vultures. The adult is quite unmistakable, having a pure white body, tail and wing coverts with a small black patch on the carpal joint (bend of the wing) and deep black primaries and secondaries; the unfeathered face is yellow as are the untidy ruff and the unusually long and pointed bill. Immatures are a dark blackish brown which gradually lightens through successive moults. At all ages, the birds can be identified in flight by the fairly long, wedged tail and the long, pointed head.

*Habitat:* Sand or stony desert, nesting on rocky ledges.

*Status in Central Arabia:* Resident breeding, but there are fewer of them around than might be expected.

*Status in Arabian Peninsula:* Resident breeding in most parts of the peninsula.

## GRIFFON VULTURE
*Gyps fulvus*
38–41 inches (97–104cm)
Wingspan 90–100 inches

*Identification:* The Griffon Vulture is a much larger bird with a shortish tail and very broad wings; the leading portion of the wing is almost straight and the rear has a distinct bulge. The adult, seen from below, has a pale head, tawny body and wing coverts, black primaries and secondaries and a black tail. The juvenile's body and wing coverts are paler and contrast even more strongly with the tail and flight feathers. On the ground they are tawny-buff with black tips to the wings. The long neck and the face are whitish and there is a white 'fur collar' round the neck (brown and wispy in the juvenile). The yellowish bill is short, very strong and, as usual with birds of prey, hooked at the tip.

Below: *The majesty of a Griffon Vulture in flight is captured here. This is one of the larger raptors in the region.*

Below right: *A Black Vulture. In contrast to the Griffon, this bird is very dark and less sociable with other vultures. Although this bird appears to be in active moult, note the characteristic broad wings.*

is decorated with a prominent black eyestripe and a black moustache. Underparts of juveniles are darker and the contrast is less striking.

*Habitat:* High and generally remote mountainous areas.

*Status in Arabian Peninsula:* Resident in a few parts of Hejaz and Asir and occasionally reported in Eastern Province and the northwest.

*Habitat:* On or above tall cliffs on mountains or escarpments.

*Status in Central Arabia:* Uncommon but perhaps increasing in numbers. One breeding colony is well established on a very tall cliff to the south of the Mecca Road and there may now be others.

*Status in Arabian Peninsula:* Possibly passage migrant in the southeast. Present in the Asir and UAE mountains.

## LAMMERGEIER
*Gypaetus barbatus*
40–45 inches (102–114cm)
Wingspan 104–114 inches

*Identification:* No lucky observer could remain unmoved at the sight of one of these birds at close quarters sailing out from a rocky cliffside. The charcoal grey wings are very long, narrow and pointed at the tip; the black tail is shaped like an elongated diamond; the underparts of the adult are creamy with a rufous tinge and the pale head

*Allied Species*
The **BLACK VULTURE** (*Aegypius monachus*) is an uncommon winter visitor to the northwest and to eastern parts of the peninsula. This very solitary bird has a totally black plumage. The unfeathered grey head can generally be picked out and the very short and broad tail separates it from the eagles.

The **LAPPET-FACED VULTURE** (*Torgos tracheliotus*) is an uncommon winter visitor to the central areas, the northwest, UAE and Oman. The underparts are grey and the upperparts black. The wings are also black apart from a white band along the leading edge.

Far left: *A Griffon Vulture viewed from above.*
Left: *The Bearded Vulture or Lammergeier.*

# Eagles

Eagles are very large birds of prey with broad, straight wings ending in splayed "fingers" (primaries) which are always black. On the ground their typically flat heads distinguish them from other large birds of prey.

Females are generally larger than males. The plumage of most species varies considerably according to the age of the bird and identification can prove extremely difficult.

Left: *Steppe Eagle.*
Bottom: *A juvenile Steppe Eagle.*

David Dinnell

David Dinnell

**STEPPE EAGLE**
*Aquila nepalensis*
26–30 inches (66–79cm)
Wingspan 62–67 inches

*Identification:* This large, dark tawny-coloured bird is rather untidy-looking when on the ground. An observer can generally get quite close to a sitting bird which, when it does take off, does so slowly and heavily. The legs are fully feathered; the usual powerful hooked bill is grey and there is a distinctive bright orange-yellow line above the base and another below forming a long yellow lip. This yellow lip is noticeable when the bird is in flight and is a useful feature helping identification.

*Juvenile:* The tawny wing (above and below) is pale in front and darker at the rear; the edges of the coverts are tipped with white which produces a very prominent white line dividing

Left: *Adult Steppe Eagle.*
Below: *An immature Steppe Eagle.*

the paler part of the wing from the darker; the tip of the dark tail is white as are the tips of the trailing flight feathers. From above a broad white rump is conspicuous and there is a white patch at the base of the primaries. When on the ground two bands of white are evident on the folded wing.

*Immature and sub-adult:* Through successive moults, as the bird approaches adulthood, the front portion of the wing darkens, the white on the rump and the base of the primaries lessens and that on the edge of the flight feathers and the tip of the tail disappears. The bird is left with a very thin white line along the upper wing and a thicker one below. The amount of white on the folded wing of a sitting bird gradually decreases as it approaches maturity.

*Adult:* There are almost no distinguishing features to the adult bird – it appears totally tawny in colour with a slight lightening on the nape (only visible from above). The long yellow lip is fairly prominent and helps to give the appearance of lightness in flight.

*Habitat:* Open desert, waste areas.

*Status in Central Arabia:* Winter visitor in large numbers. Observed from October until March.

*Status in Arabian Peninsula:* Appears less common away from the centre, although several have been reported in the desert areas of Eastern Province and they are present in small numbers in most parts of the peninsula during the winter months.

David Dinnell

Above: *Immature Steppe Eagle showing the white rump contrasting with the dark tail. The yellow 'lip' of the bill can also be seen.*

27

## IMPERIAL EAGLE
*Aquila heliaca*
31–33 inches (78–84cm)
Wingspan 70–75 inches

*Identification:* Although the Imperial Eagle is larger than the Steppe Eagle, unless one is fortunate enough to see the two species flying close to one another, this is not a useful guide. Imperials, however, do not possess the yellow lip of the Steppes.

The plumage of juveniles and, to a lesser extent, immatures is distinctive enough to make identification fairly easy. From below they do not have the white line dividing coverts from primaries and secondaries; the body is brownish-ochre and clearly streaked darker, as are the wing coverts. The primaries and secondaries are blackish but there is a distinct lightening at the base of the primaries which gives the wing an appearance of being broken between the black splayed "fingers" and the black of the flight feathers. Juveniles show a narrow white edge to the tail and trailing flight feathers. From above a narrow white line can be seen at the base of the coverts which broadens to form a semi-circular patch at the base of the primaries. During the transitional plumages of immaturity all these features gradually disappear. The bird takes six years to reach maturity. The adult bird is blackish-brown with a pale crown and nape, pale base to the tail and shows white spots on the shoulders.

*Habitat:* Desert country with nearby cliffs and occasionally on waste areas.

*Status in Central Arabia:* Uncommon winter visitor.

*Status in Arabian Peninsula:* Uncommon passage migrant to Gulf Coast areas.

Centre top: *Imperial Eagle. This juvenile shows the pale bases to the primaries that are a useful field mark.*

## LESSER SPOTTED EAGLE
*Aquila pomarina*
24–26 inches (66–79cm)
Wingspan 55–64 inches

*Identification:* It is difficult to distinguish this bird from the Steppe Eagle although the tail of the Lesser Spotted is shorter and wider at the base – there is also a pale patch near the base of the under side of the tail. The coverts are chocolate brown, the secondaries and primaries black. Juveniles show a white 'V' on the rump and a very narrow – and short – white line in the centre of the upper wing.

*Habitat:* Generally not too far from water or damp ground.

*Status in Central Arabia:* Uncommon passage migrant.

*Lesser Spotted Eagle. Note the relatively short tail.*

*Status in Arabian Peninsula:* Uncommon passage migrant – reported occasionally in several parts of the peninsula, as is the Spotted Eagle (*Aquila clanga*).

## OSPREY
*Pandion haliaetus*
20–23 inches (51–58cm)
Wingspan 58–64 inches

*Identification:* Observed perched on a post or the edge of a rocky cliff this bird is unmistakable. The upperparts, wings and tail are blackish-brown; the underparts and the crown and nape are white and a broad dark line runs up the side of the neck to meet the pale blue eye. In flight, seen from above, the bird is dark apart from the white crown; from below it is pure white on the underparts and wing coverts, pale grey on flight feathers and tail and has a conspicuous dark patch on the carpal joint. The Osprey (or Fish Hawk) feeds mainly on fish. It will sail from its perch, hover gently and then dive into the water to catch its prey.

*Habitat:* Coastal areas and near large expanses of inland water.

*Status in Central Arabia:* Rare migrant.

*Status in Arabian Peninsula:* Breeds in small numbers in Hejaz and along the Gulf Coast.

*Other Eagles*
**BONELLI'S EAGLE** (*Hieraaetus fasciatus*) has very occasionally been observed in central Arabia, Asir, Kuwait and UAE. The adult has an unmistakable broad black band running along the underside of the wing. The line is narrower in immature birds.

The **BOOTED EAGLE** (*Hieraaetus pennatus*) has an almost identical status as Bonelli's. This bird has two phases, one pale and the other dark. It is almost invariably seen in the dark phase over Arabia; this is chocolate brown, darkening on flight feathers and a rufous tail. In its pale phase the bird has a whitish body, undertail and underwing coverts which contrast strongly with its dark flight feathers.

The **WHITE-TAILED EAGLE** (*Haliaeetus albicilla*) is an uncommon winter visitor to the Gulf Coast and Oman. This dark brown bird has a paler brown head and nape and a basically white tail with dark brown at basal centre.

Left: *An Osprey searching for fish.*
Above: *Osprey.*

# Buzzards

Buzzards can be distinguished from the eagles when on the ground by their much rounder heads and when in the air by their less protruding heads, shorter and more rounded wings and by the very much shorter primaries (the 'splayed fingers' mentioned when discussing the eagles).

## LONG-LEGGED BUZZARD
*Buteo rufinus*
20–26 inches (51–66cm)
Wingspan 52–63 inches

*Identification:* Underparts and wing coverts are palish chestnut-brown with two distinct crescent-shaped patches on the carpal joints; the primaries and secondaries are whitish with black tips and edges; the tail is unbarred and pale chestnut in colour. Upperparts are very variable in depth of brown.

*Habitat:* Rocky cliffs and escarpments. Whereas eagles will perch only on posts or tree trunks, this bird can be seen perched on telegraph wires and the topmost branches of trees.

*Status in Central Arabia:* Uncertain. Isolated birds have been observed during winter months and in late spring and early summer they seem to be present in greater numbers. It is possible that they breed in one or two places near the Tuwaiq escarpment.

*Status in Arabian Peninsula:* Breeds in Hejaz, Asir, the northwest and along the Gulf Coast. Winter visitor and passage migrant in greater numbers.

The **BUZZARD** (*Buteo buteo*) has occasionally been reported over the central regions and is a passage migrant to most parts of the peninsula. Its plumage varies greatly from pale to dark, the tail is generally lightly barred and there are dark patches on the carpal joints.

Right: *The Long-legged Buzzard is the true desert Buzzard of the area; the others all have ranges extending well into Europe.*

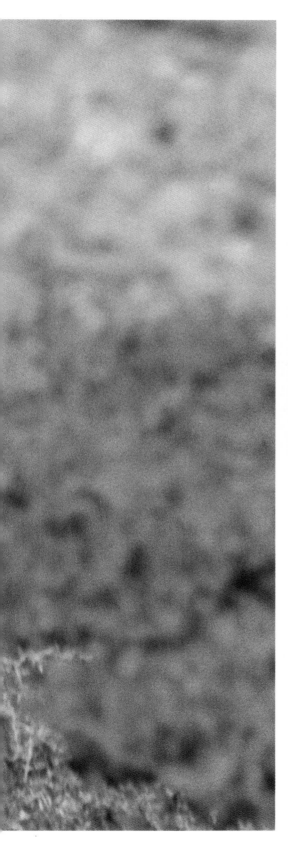

Above: *A Long-legged Buzzard leaves its perch.*
Right: *A Honey Buzzard.*

## HONEY BUZZARD
*Pernis apivorus*
20–23 inches (51–58cm)
Wingspan 47–50 inches

*Identification:* The Honey Buzzard is best distinguished from the Buteo buzzards by its longer and more protruding head and by the presence of two dark bars near the base of the tail as well as a broader one at the tip. Once again the plumage is very variable. The underparts and the wing coverts are generally dark (often with a darker patch on the carpal joint); the primaries and secondaries are paler (often almost white) with black on the tips of the primaries and along the trailing edge of the wing. On the ground its posture is often nearly horizontal.

*Habitat:* Well-treed areas.

*Status in Arabian Peninsula:* Passage migrant in very small numbers to mountainous areas of Asir and UAE.

Top: *Black Kite. The forked tail of the adult is probably the best field mark of this distinctive bird.*
Above: *An immature Black Kite perches on telegraph wires.*
Right: *Marsh Harrier. The Harriers may be distinguished from the Kites by the shallow 'V' shape in which they hold their wings.*

## BLACK KITE
*Milvus migrans*
22 inches (56cm)
Wingspan 44 inches

*Identification:* The Black Kite is best distinguished from other birds of prey of the area by its slightly forked tail. However, the forked tail is not always readily visible in flight and probably the wing shape, tail length and dark colour are more immediately identifiable. Its general appearance in flight is dark blackish-brown, the leading half of the wing being generally darker than the rear; head and tail are paler and there is a variable pale patch on the base of the primaries. Flight is vigorous and, when gliding, the wings are held in a shallow arch. The plumage of juveniles and immatures is very variable indeed, some being more rufous than others but they are all fairly heavily streaked.

*Habitat:* Most types of country but generally near water.

*Status in Central Arabia:* Only present as uncommon migrants.

*Status in Arabian Peninsula:* Common resident breeding in Hejaz and Asir. Less common migrant and winter visitor on the Gulf Coast.

## MARSH HARRIER
*Circus aeruginosus*
20 inches (50cm)
Wingspan 44–49 inches

*Identification:* The adult male differs from other harriers in having a tri-coloured plumage; the body and wing coverts (above and below) are rusty-brown (paling as the bird ages); the primaries are broadly tipped black and the remainder of the wing and the tail are grey. The female is dark blackish-brown apart from the head and the leading edge of the wings which are pale cream. Immatures are dark with just a little lightening on the head and forewing. When gliding the wings are always raised in a shallow 'V'. These birds are seldom seen flying high but are generally observed flying low over marsh land or reed-filled lakes and lagoons.

*Habitat:* Marshes and lakes with plenty of vegetation.

*Status in Central Arabia:* Winter visitor.

*Status in Arabian Peninsula:* Winter visitor in th southwest and Eastern Province.

*Allied Specie*
The **PALLID HARRIER** (*Circus macrourus*) is a winter visitor throughout the peninsula in fairly small numbers. The male is soft, pale grey (some almost white) with black central primaries. Females and immatures are similar to the Marsh but are without the pale head and forewing; they have a narrow white rump and a barred tail.

## SPARROWHAWK
*Accipiter nisus*
11–15 inches (28–38cm)
Wingspan 24–31 inches

*Identification:* The hawks can be separated from other birds of prey by their long tails and short, wide rounded wings. Females are larger than males. The upperparts of the Sparrowhawk are dark brownish-grey; underparts are distinctly barred across breast and belly (rufous on the male and dark brown on the female). In flight the barring on the body is continued along the underwing. The tail is barred on both sides.

*Habitat:* Wooded areas.

*Status in Central Arabia:* Uncommon autumn migrant and winter visitor.

*Status in Arabian Peninsula:* Passage migrant and winter visitor in Asir and eastern parts of the peninsula.

Top right: *A female Marsh Harrier showing the pale crown.*
Right: *Sparrowhawk.*

Betty Vincett

*Allied Species*
The much bigger **GOSHAWK** (*Accipiter gentilis*) is an uncommon winter visitor to Eastern Province and UAE. Apart from its greater size and white undertail coverts it is very similar to the Sparrowhawk.

The **CHANTING GOSHAWK** (*Melierax metabates*) is a winter visitor to western parts of the peninsula. It can be distinguished from other hawks by its unstreaked throat and upper breast, by much finer barring on the rest of the underparts and by having red legs and red at the base of the bill.

**FALCONS** (*Falconidae*). The larger members of this family are among the most favoured for the ancient sport of falconry. One of the fascinating things to see in this part of the world is a falconer training a young bird – the patience and dedication shown is truly remarkable. To see a large hooded bird on the wrist of a cloaked Arab brings a touch of romance to any scene and one of the most interesting parts of an Arabian *Suq* (market) is undoubtedly the place where falcons are offered for sale. With one or two exceptions the large falcons do not breed in the peninsula (except in captivity) though the **SAKER** and the **PEREGRINE** (*Falco cherrug* and *Falco peregrinus*) are winter visitors and passage migrants in eastern areas. The **LANNER FALCON** (*Falco biarmicus*) breeds in Eastern Province and elsewhere along the Gulf; it is also occasionally seen in the centre and it is just possible that it may breed there in very small numbers. The **SOOTY FALCON** (*Falco concolor*) is a migrant breeder in eastern parts of the Gulf and in Bahrain; it is also faintly possible that it breeds in one or two isolated rocky areas elsewhere. The **BARBARY FALCON** (*Falco pelegrinoides*) almost certainly breeds high up on an isolated cliff south of Riyadh off the Mecca Road and is possibly also doing so in one or two other similar localities. Its raucous scream can be heard as it darts from its shelter to warn off an approaching raven, vulture or eagle.

Falcons can be recognised by their long narrow pointed wings and longish tails. The wings are often held straight back from the carpal joint.

### KESTREL
*Falco tinnunculus*
$13\frac{1}{2}$ inches (34cm)

*Identification:* This smaller member of the falcon family can commonly be seen in almost all parts of the peninsula. The male has a grey head, grey tail tipped with black, chestnut mantle and upperwing coverts both markedly spotted black and pale underparts also spotted black. In flight

*Falconry is still a popular sport in Saudi Arabia. Here, a group of falcons are offered for sale in the* suq.

Heather Ross

David Dinnell

he shows very pale, almost white, underparts and underwing which are both delicately marked with black; from above his unbarred grey tail, rump and crown, chestnut mantle and wing coverts are in marked contrast to the black flight feathers. The female is reddish-brown above and on the tail and wing coverts, all of which are well spotted with black; the tips of her wings are black and underparts are pale with black spots. Both sexes have distinct black lachrymal stripes down the side of the face below the eye. Its habit of almost continual hovering makes it particularly easy to identify.

*Habitat:* Almost anywhere, particularly near cultivation.

*Status in Central Arabia:* Uncommon breeder, more common winter visitor and passage migrant.

*Female Kestrel.*

*Status in Arabian Peninsula:* Resident breeding, winter visitor and passage migrant to most areas.

## LESSER KESTREL
*Falco naumanni*
12 inches (30cm)

*Identification:* The male can be separated from the ordinary Kestrel by his unspotted chestnut mantle and blue-grey upperwing coverts. The females of both species are almost identical except that the Lesser does not have black claws and has a less-pronounced lachrymal stripe (the male Lesser is completely without one). In flight these birds hover less frequently, spending more time gliding.

*Habitat:* Similar to Kestrel.

*Status in Arabian Peninsula:* Passage migrant to almost all areas.

Above: *Female Lesser Kestrel.*

*Allied specie*
The **HOBBY** (*Falco subbuteo*) is a passage migrant to most areas, though not commonly seen in the central region. Its long arched wings give it similarity to a swift in flight. Upperparts are dark, all underparts are heavily streaked dark on white except for an unstreaked white throat and deep chestnut on undertail coverts and thighs.

Top: *Male Kestrel.*

# Owls

These birds are nocturnal birds of prey and, since they are very rarely to be seen during daylight hours, are thus almost impossible to photograph. They have prominent eyes, generally set in the widely-depicted facial disc. They have long rounded wings, feathered legs and feet (except for the Barn Owl) and, in flight, the flattened front to the head is an almost infallible aid to identification.

Mike Jennings

Above: *Little Owl.*

The **LITTLE OWL** (*Athene noctua*) is present in most parts of the peninsula and, due to its occasional daytime appearances, it is the most likely to be spotted. Its upperparts are dark brown, spotted white; underparts are white, streaked black. Its flight is unusually bounding and its flattened head and short tail make it easy to identify. (8½ inches/22cm).

**HUME'S TAWNY OWL** (*Strix butleri*) is reliably reported to breed in very small numbers in rocky wadis and cliffs in central Arabia and Asir. It is a pale tawny owl with large beady black eyes. (15 inches/38cm).

Centre and right: *Hume's Tawny Owl. This is a race of the European Tawny Owl, that has evolved pale plumage for camouflage in the desert.*

Mike Jennings

Mike Jennings

The **EAGLE OWL** (*Bubo bubo*) breeds in the eastern parts of the peninsula. It is the largest of the owls found in the area, has long pointed "ears" and bright orange eyes. (26–28 inches/56–61cm).

**SCOPS OWL** (*Otus scops*) is a winter visitor and passage migrant to most parts of the peninsula. It is a small grey bird with narrow black streaks, a chequerboard pattern on the edge of the folded wing and it has short 'ear' tufts (8 inches/20cm). **BRUCE'S SCOPS OWL** (*Otus brucei*) is a paler and slightly larger version (8½ inches/22cm) which breeds in the mountains of the UAE.

The **BARN OWL** (*Tyto alba*) is present in its dark-breasted phase in Hejaz and in areas round the Gulf Coast. It is generally rufous in colour, well-spotted on its mantle and wings and with a very prominent white facial disc (14 inches/36cm).

Above: *Scops Owl. This slim little owl is only a visitor to Saudi Arabia. Its call is a soft 'mew' which may betray its presence.*

*Grey Heron*, Ardea cinerea.

This chapter purports to describe the birds of the peninsula which are only found beside water and which are *not* classed as waders.

# Herons and Egrets (Ardeidae)

Herons and egrets are large to very large waterside birds with long necks and long legs. In flight the wings are broad and rounded, the legs trail and the neck is retracted – as it is on occasions on the ground. Sexes are generally alike.

Centre right: *The Grey Heron, a winter visitor to Saudi Arabia, is the largest of the Arabian herons.*
Below: *A purple Heron in the hand.*

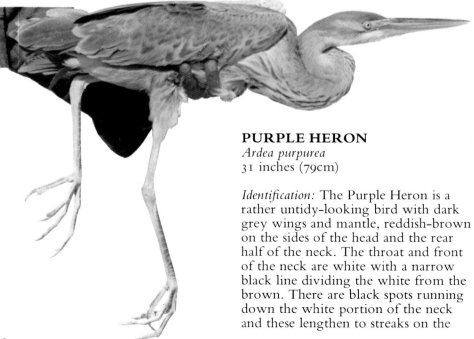

## GREY HERON
*Ardea cinerea*
36 inches (90cm)

*Identification:* This heron has a soft grey mantle and wings, a near-white head, neck and belly with a double line of short black streaks running down the front of the neck. There is a narrow black crest trailing from a black stripe behind the yellow eye; the legs are yellowish-grey as is the strong straight bill. They are solitary birds, except during nesting season, and will stand like statues for long periods. In flight the very slow wingbeat is distinctive and so is the sharp demarcation line bisecting the upperwing, with the inner and front portion pale grey and the outer and rear portion very dark grey, almost black.

*Habitat:* In or beside shallow salt or fresh water. Nests are in trees.

*Status in Central Arabia:* Winter visitor and passage migrant.

*Status in Arabian Peninsula:* Has been known to breed in Kuwait. Winter visitor and passage migrant to most other parts of the peninsula.

## PURPLE HERON
*Ardea purpurea*
31 inches (79cm)

*Identification:* The Purple Heron is a rather untidy-looking bird with dark grey wings and mantle, reddish-brown on the sides of the head and the rear half of the neck. The throat and front of the neck are white with a narrow black line dividing the white from the brown. There are black spots running down the white portion of the neck and these lengthen to streaks on the breast. The crown is black, there are black and white stripes along the side of the face and a narrow black crest droops from the black crown. In flight the whole wing, above and below, is a very dark grey with a rufous tinge to the forewing. The bulge of the retracted neck is more pronounced than in the Grey. The juvenile is rufous-brown with heavy dark brown streaking.

*Habitat:* Beside permanent water with tall, thick cover.

*Status in Central Arabia:* Passage migrant. More juveniles are seen than adults.

*Status in Arabian Peninsula:* Has been known to breed in Kuwait. Uncommon passage migrant in most other areas.

Below: *The Squacco Heron is one of the smallest Arabian herons.*
Bottom: *Little Egret.*

## SQUACCO HERON
*Ardeola ralloides*
18 inches (46cm)

*Identification:* This much smaller heron is unusual in that its appearance when on the wing is quite different to that when on the ground. On the ground it appears tawny-brown (in autumn migration) or yellowish-buff (in the spring). In flight the white wings, belly and tail transform it into a white bird with brown or buff on neck and mantle. Juveniles are darker with blackish streaks down head and neck – their wings, belly and tail are as white as the adults.

*Habitat:* Coastal areas and by inland water with plenty of cover.

*Status in Central Arabia:* Passage migrant and less common summer visitor.

*Status in Arabian Peninsula:* Possibly now breeding in UAE; passage migrant in most other areas.

## LITTLE EGRET
*Egretta garzetta*
22 inches (56cm)

*Identification:* The Little Egret is a pure white heron with black bill, black legs and yellow feet; the yellow feet can be difficult to spot when on the ground but they are fairly conspicuous in flight. In breeding season long white plumes protrude from the back of the head, from the breast and from the wings. These were once in great demand as 'osprey' feathers.

*Habitat:* Generally near inland water.

*Status in Central Arabia:* Passage migrant.

*Status in Arabian Peninsula:* Winter visitor and passage migrant to almost all areas.

41

## GREAT WHITE EGRET
*Egretta alba*
35 inches (88cm)

*Identification:* The Great White Egret is another pure white heron but is very much larger (much the same as a Grey Heron) than the Little Egret. The legs and feet are black; the colour of the bill is variable – it can be yellow or black or yellow at the base and black at the tip. They have no crest.

*Habitat:* By coastal or inland water.

*Status in Central Arabia:* Uncommon passage migrant.

*Status in Arabian Peninsula:* Winter visitor and passage migrant to Hejaz, Eastern Province, Bahrain and Oman.

## YELLOW–BILLED EGRET
*Egretta intermedia*
26 inches (66cm)

*Identification:* The Yellow–Billed Egret is a very sleek and graceful pure white bird with a fairly short yellow bill, black legs and black feet. It is larger than the Cattle, with which it can be confused, and never has the touch of apricot on the crown which the Cattle Egret invariably has.

*Habitat:* By salt or fresh water.

*Status in Central Arabia:* Rare passage migrant. A flock of five was observed by the author in October at the sewage lagoon and a pair was reported by a waterhole near Muzamiyah in November.

*Status in Arabian Peninsula:* Rare passage migrant to Hejaz, the Gulf Coast and Bahrain.

## CATTLE EGRET
*Bubulcus ibis*
20 inches (51cm)

*Identification:* Except during the breeding season, this bird is white with a touch of apricot on the forehead. Breeding plumage includes wispy

Opposite: *A Great White Heron scratches and shows the black feet that distinguishes it from some other species.*

Below: *Yellow–Billed Egret.*
Bottom: *Cattle Egret feeding in low scrubby vegetation.*

apricot plumes on crown, breast and wings. The bill is yellow, legs and feet are greenish-grey (reddish during breeding).

*Habitat:* Almost always near cattle or other livestock but on migration will land near water.

*Status in Central Arabia:* Uncommon passage migrant.

*Status in Arabian Peninsula:* Uncommon passage migrant to Hejaz, the northwest, Eastern Province and UAE.

Betty Vincett

43

Below: *Reef Heron in dark phase plumage.*

Bottom: *A light phase Reef Heron showing yellow feet.*

## REEF HERON
*Egretta gularis*
22 inches (56cm)

*Identification:* This small heron can be either all white *or* very dark grey, almost black. Both phases have black legs, yellow feet and horn-coloured bills. Generally seen feeding in fairly deep coastal water where it strides along in a business-like fashion, sometimes breaking into a run with wings outstretched. During the breeding season there are narrow plumes on the back of the head.

*Habitat:* Coastal areas and inland salt-water lagoons.

*Status in Arabian Peninsula:* Resident breeding in Oman, UAE and Bahrain. Winter visitor and passage migrant to Hejaz and Eastern Province. Black phase appears to predominate in the eastern coastal areas.

*Allied Species*
The very large **GOLIATH HERON** (*Ardea goliath*) (47 inches/120cm) has been reliably reported on a few occasions in the northwest of Saudi Arabia. Its colouring is very similar to the Purple but it lacks the black and white on the head.

The **LITTLE BITTERN** (*Ixobrychus minutus*) is a passage migrant and winter visitor in most parts of the peninsula east of the central region and in the northwest. It is reported to breed in Eastern Province. The male is black and buff with prominent buff on the shoulder which is conspicuous in flight. The female is brown with a less conspicuous wing patch. When

alarmed they 'point', standing erect with neck extended and bill aimed at the sky.

The much larger **BITTERN** (*Botaurus stellaris*) is a winter visitor and passage migrant in small numbers in eastern

44

parts of the peninsula. It is brown, heavily speckled black and has a black crown. It, too, will 'point' when alarmed.

The black, grey and white **NIGHT HERON** (*Nyctiocorax nycticorax*) is a fairly common migrant in the Khassim district of central Arabia and along the eastern parts of the peninsula.

## GLOSSY IBIS
*Plegadis falcinellus*
22 inches (56cm)

*Identification:* The Glossy Ibis is a tall bird, dark reddish brown on neck and mantle with dark greenish-black wings; both colours become irridescent in sunlight. The long, black bill is down-curved and the legs are greenish. In flight the legs protrude a little and birds generally fly in line.

*Habitat:* Beside permanent water.

*Status in Central Arabia:* Rare passage migrant.

*Status in Arabian Peninsula:* Passage migrant and winter visitor in Hejaz, the northwest and Eastern Province.

*Allied Specie*
The **SPOONBILL** (*Platalea leucorodia*) has bred in Kuwait and is a winter visitor and passage migrant to Hejaz, Oman and the Gulf Coast. It is a white bird with a yellowish breast and, in breeding season, a drooping yellow crest. The legs are black and the broad black bill is spoon-shaped at the tip.

Above: *Bittern.*
Below: *The Glossy Ibis is one of the most distinctive birds of Heron size. In poor light it might be confused with the Curlew (page 60). The Ibis has a shorter bill.*

## HAMERKOP
*Scopus umbretta*
22 inches (56cm)

*Identification:* The hamerkop is a totally dusky-brown bird with a broad crest which gives it a uniquely shaped head and provides its name 'hammerhead'. It has an exceptionally thick, black bill and is generally hunched up when on the ground. In flight the head is extended, the wings are broad and it flies slowly. The voice is loud and strident. It is distantly related to storks and to herons.

*Habitat:* Almost always near water.

*Status in Arabian Peninsula:* Possibly uncommon resident in lower parts of Asir; migrant to Hejaz.

Above: *The Hamerkop is a strange relative of the storks and herons.*

*Other large waterside birds*
The **WHITE STORK** (*Ciconia ciconia*) is an uncommon passage migrant in Hejaz and along the Gulf Coast. It is a very large bird and is white all over apart from the flight feathers which are black. The long legs and the heavy bill are red.

The **BLACK STORK** (*Ciconia nigra*) is an uncommon migrant to eastern parts of the peninsula. It is totally black apart from its belly and undertail coverts which are white. The bill and legs are red.

The **GREATER FLAMINGO** (*Phoenicopterus ruber*) has been reported in almost every part of the peninsula, including the centre. This bird, with its long red legs and very long snake-like neck, is pale pinky-white with deep pink wing coverts and black primaries and secondaries. It is reported to have bred in Kuwait and is a winter visitor and passage migrant elsewhere.

---

## SPOTTED CRAKE
*Porzana porzana*
9 inchs (23cm)

*Identification:* Basically brown in colour, the Spotted Crake is heavily spotted with white, with long greenish legs and very long toes. It has a very short tail which is frequently cocked to show fawn undertail coverts.

*Habitat:* Skulking on sand or muddy flats beside permanent water. They appear to exhaust themselves very suddenly as, on one or two occasions, they have crashed into the wall of a house or garden and knocked themselves out. The skulking habits of this bird make it very difficult to find unless it calls.

*Status in Central Arabia:* Uncommon (or perhaps just very hard to spot) passage migrant.

*Status in Arabian Peninsula:* Passage migrant in the east.

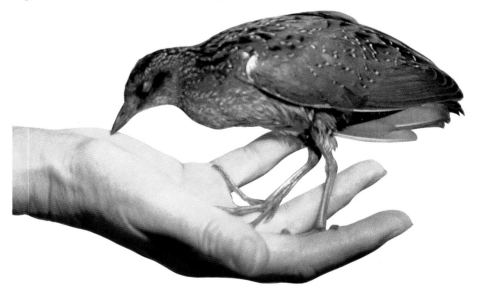

Above: *Spotted Crake.*

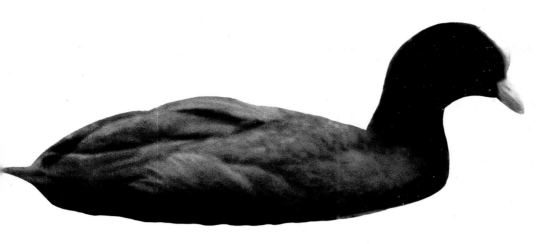

Above: *Coot.*

## COOT
*Fulica atra*
15 inches (38cm)

*Identification:* This waterfowl is completely black except for a white forehead and bill and a white wingbar which only shows in flight. Juveniles are dark grey, lighter on the throat and on the front of the neck. It take-off and flight are as laboured as those of the Moorhen.

*Habitat:* Identical to Moorhen.

*Status in Central Arabia:* Winter visitor.

*Status in Arabian Peninsula:* Resident breeding in Eastern Province; winter visitor and passage migrant to the northwest and Bahrain.

## MOORHEN
*Gallinula chloropus*
13 inches (33cm)

*Identification:* The Moorhen is a black waterfowl with red eyes, red bill and red forehead. The undertail coverts are pure white and are very conspicuous as the tail is constantly flicked. There is also a thin line of white along the flank. It swims with a jerky movement of the head and will dive. When flushed it takes some time to raise the trailing legs and will almost run on the water with frantically beating wings before it manages to get airborne. Juveniles lack the red on the face and have a grey plumage.

*Habitat:* On and beside fresh water with thick reed cover.

*Status in Arabian Peninsula:* Resident breeding in almost all areas.

*Allied Species*
The **WATER RAIL** (*Rallus aquaticus*) is present in most parts of the east. It is brown, streaked black above and grey below with black and white stripes on the flanks and prominent white undertail coverts. A very skulking bird that is seldom seen.

**BUSTARDS** (*Otididae*). There are two members of this genus found in the peninsula but they are both becoming dangerously close to extinction. A very small number of **ARABIAN BUSTARDS** (*Ardeotis arabs*) is still to be found in Asir; this very large bird is grey on its head and long neck, brown on the mantle, tail and wing and is white on the belly. There is a short crest at the back of the head and a distinct white stripe above the eye.

The **HOUBARA BUSTARD** (*Chlamydotis undulata*) is occasionally reported in various low-lying areas. It is believed still to breed in Kuwait and in Eastern Province and is a very uncommon winter visitor elsewhere. It is smaller than the Arabian, has a less conspicuous, drooping crest and a line of black running down the side of the neck; otherwise the plumage of the two species is very similar.

Right: *Moorhen.*

47

This large group of birds is divided into many families. Here, apart from the large waders described on this page, they will be divided into two groups: first plovers and second sandpipers and snipe. They are always found near water (salt or fresh) or on marshy ground. Almost all are gregarious and, especially in winter, can be seen in large flocks flying and wheeling in concert.

## BLACK-WINGED STILT
*Himantopus himantopus*
15 inches (38cm)

*Identification:* This very delicate, almost brittle-looking bird has incredibly long thin red legs. The mantle and both sides of the wing are black (slightly brownish in the female) and the rest of the body is pure white, except that the breeding male has a dark grey crown and nape. The black bill is long, very thin and pointed and the eyes are black. In flight the long red legs trail behind and provide an unmistakable identification feature.

*Habitat:* Beside permanent water.

*Status in Central Arabia:* Uncommon passage migrant.

*Status in Arabian Peninsula:* Passage migrant to Hejaz, Eastern Province and Oman. Now breeding in small numbers in Eastern Province and Abu Dhabi.

## The OYSTERCATCHER
(*Haematopus ostralegu*) visits most of the coastal areas during winter months and groups of up to 80 birds can be seen in the spring. This heavy-looking bird is black on mantle, wings, head and breast but is white below. Legs are bright pink and the eyes and long bill are red. In flight the black upperwing shows a broad white bar and the underwing is totally white.

The **CRAB PLOVER** (*Dromas ardeola*) breeds in Kuwait and is an uncommon migrant to Hejaz and Oman. Its head and underparts are

Frank Naylor

white, the wings are black and white and there is a very heavy-looking black bill.

# Plovers

Plovers form a group of small to medium-sized waders with characteristic short stubby bills and with differing distinctive black and white head patterns which, in most cases, are lacking during winter months. The sexes are generally alike.

## RINGED PLOVER
*Charadrius hiaticula*
7½ inches (19cm)

*Identification:* For the greater part of the year this medium-small plover is brown above and white below with a black breast-band below a white collar; there is a broad black eyestripe which divides over the forehead to show a narrow white band above the

base of the bill. The legs and the bill are yellow/orange. During early winter months the birds lose their distinctive head pattern and, apart from their yellow legs, are difficult to distinguish from other similar waders. In flight the trailing edge of the wing

Left: *A group of Black-winged Stilts.*

Below: *Little Ringed Plover.*

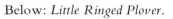

Below left: *Ringed plover in winter plumage.*
Below right: *A Ringed Plover in summer plumage.*

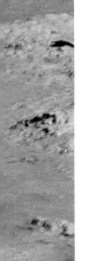

is black and there is a white bar dividing this from the brown coverts; the upperside of the tail is black.

*Habitat:* Mainly by the seashore but also beside stretches of inland water with sandy banks.

*Status in Central Arabia:* Winter visitor.

*Status in Arabian Peninsula:* Winter visitor and passage migrant to most coastal areas.

## LITTLE RINGED PLOVER
*Charadrius dubius*
6 inches (15cm)

*Identification:* The Little Ringed Plover is similar to the Ringed but it is not too difficult to distinguish them. The white band on the forehead of the Little Ringed is broader in summer, the bill is black and the legs yellowish-grey. In flight there is no black on the tail and no wing bar. In winter the smaller size, the lack of a white eye-stripe and less white on the forehead are aids to identification.

*Habitat:* Beside shallow *inland* water.

*Status in Central Arabia:* Although no positive evidence of breeding is to hand it becomes increasingly certain that a few pairs are in fact doing so. Isolated pairs have been observed in one or two localised spots in almost all months of the year.

*Status in Arabian Peninsula:* Passage migrant in fairly small numbers to Hejaz and Eastern Province.

## KENTISH PLOVER
*Charadrius alexandrinus*
6 inches (15cm)

*Identification:* The Kentish Plover is a paler brown than the two Ringed Plovers with less black on the head. In summer the male has a pale chestnut crown, a black stripe behind the eye, a black spot above the white forehead and a black spot on the shoulder. Its bill and legs are dark grey to black. The female and winter male are very similar to other small plovers in winter dress though the fairly distinct darkish spot on the shoulder, the eyestripe and the black legs are a help. In flight the wing pattern is similar to the Ringed but there is less black on the tail.

*Habitat:* Mainly coastal areas though occasionally beside shallow inland water.

*Status in Central Arabia:* Uncommon winter visitor.

*Status in Arabian Peninsula:* Winter visitor and passage migrant to most coastal areas, breeding in Eastern Province and UAE.

## GREATER SAND PLOVER
*Charadrius leschenaultii*
10 inches (25cm)

*Identification:* The Greater Sand Plover is a large plover which dwarfs the Ringed and Kentish in whose company it can often be found. In winter it is a nondescript grey-brown above with black at the edge of the folded wing; the brown extends round the shoulder to almost meet below the throat; underparts are white; the short bill is black; the eyes are black and there is a black spot in front of them; the long legs are grey-green. In summer the nape, breast-band and a narrow line above a broad black eyestripe all turn chestnut. The black eyestripe continues across the forehead, a narrow black line drops from the eye to each side of the bill and there is quite a broad area of white within these lines above the bill. In flight the tips of the wing are dark, there is a

Left: *Kentish Plover in winter plumage.*
Below: *Kentish Plover in summer plumage.*
Bottom: *Greater Sand Plover on passage in March showing transitional plumage between summer and winter.*

short white wing bar and the central tail feathers are black and the outer ones white.

*Habitat:* By the edge of coastal water and occasionally beside fresh water lagoons.

*Status in Central Arabia:* Passage migrant in small numbers.

*Status in Arabian Peninsula:* Winter visitor and passage migrant to most coastal areas.

## GREY PLOVER
*Pluvialis squatarola*
11 inches (28cm)

*Identification:* This plover can be distinguished in all plumages by the quite large black patches on its wingpits which are very conspicuous when the bird is in flight. In winter the crown, mantle, wings and tail are well-speckled grey-brown, blackish and white and the breast is streaked brownish-grey. The throat and belly are white and there is a white eyestripe. In summer the lower half of the face and the entire underparts (apart from white undertail coverts) turn black and the upperparts are speckled black and white.

*Habitat:* Sand banks and sandy beaches. Occasionally found on similar edges of inland water.

*Status in Central Arabia:* Rare passage migrant.

*Status in Arabian Peninsula:* Winter visitor and passage migrant to most coastal areas.

## TURNSTONE
*Arenaria interpres*
9 inches (23cm)

*Identification:* In summer this bird is dark brown, reddish brown and black on the upperparts and white below with an extensive black bib. In flight the very intricate pattern of brown, white and black is unmistakable. In winter the upperparts are mottled brownish-grey and the black bib less extensive. The legs are orange and the black bill is pointed and slightly upturned at the tip which enables it to topple over small stones in search of food – hence its name.

*Habitat:* Generally on stony, sea-weedy beaches, but large flocks were observed on the mud flats at Jeddah at low tide. Very occasionally found beside inland water.

*Status in Central Arabia:* Uncommon passage migrant.

*Status in Arabian Peninsula:* Commonly seen in both plumages in most coastal areas.

*Allied Species*
## The LESSER SAND PLOVER
(*Charadrius mongolus*) is an uncommon winter visitor and passage migrant to some areas of the Gulf Coast and Oman. In winter it is very similar to the Greater Sand but has a white stripe above the eye. In summer the chestnut on the breast is more extensive. In flight the short wingbar is very indistinct and there is more black in the centre of the upper tail.

The **GOLDEN PLOVER** (*Pluvius apricaria*) is an uncommon winter visitor and passage migrant to Eastern Province, the Gulf Coast and Oman. It is very similar in both plumages to the Grey but the upperparts of the Golden are speckled yellow-brown and black and are conspicuously bordered with white in the summer. This bird does not have the conspicuous black patches on the wingpits.

Below: *Lesser Sand Plover.*
Bottom: *The Turnstone is another visitor from Europe.*

Left: *The Grey Plover, here shown in winter plumage, is a migrant from northern Europe.*

Top: *A pair of Lapwings.*

Above: *Lapwing.*

## Sandpipers

Sandpipers are small to medium-large waders generally with long slender bills.

### LITTLE STINT
*Calidris minuta*
5¼ inches (13cm)

*Identification:* In winter plumage this very small little wader is mottled greyish-brown above and white below. In summer the upperparts take on a more reddish tinge but remain markedly mottled. The bill and the short legs are always black. In flight the grey wings have a narrow white bar and the tail and rump are black in the centre with grey at the sides.

*Habitat:* Salt or fresh water.

*Status in Central Arabia:* Observed in all months of the year with an increase in numbers in spring and autumn. Possibly now breeding.

### LAPWING
*Vanellus vanellus*
12 inches (30cm)

*Identification:* The Lapwing is a much larger wader that is one of a different genus, all of which have broadly tipped black wings. The mantle and wings are black, appearing greenish in sunlight; there is a broad black bib extending to cover the throat and, its most distinctive feature, a prominent back-swept crest arcs high above the head. In flight the bird appears all black from above apart from white on the face and on the rump; from below it is white with a black throat, a black tip on its tail and black flight feathers. In flight and on the ground the apricot undertail coverts are fairly conspicuous. Its cry of 'pee-wit' gives it the name by which it is familiarly known in Great Britain.

*Habitat:* By permanent inland water or on marshy land.

*Status throughout the Peninsula:* Uncommon passage migrant and winter visitor to the centre, the northwest and Eastern Province.

*Allied Species*
The **RED-WATTLED LAPWING** (*Vanellus indicus*) breeds in UAE and Oman, is a passage migrant to Gulf Coast areas and an occasional visitor to the centre. The mantle and wings are brown; the crown, throat, breast, tail and wing tips are black; the bill is red tipped black. There is a red circle round the eye and a prominent red wattle round the forehead.

The **WHITE-TAILED LAPWING** (*Vanellus leucurus*) is an uncommon migrant to the northwest and the Gulf Coast. It is brown above and cream below with a greyish breast. The wings are tipped black, the bill is black, the long legs are yellow and the tail is white.

### DUNLIN
*Calidris alpina*
7 inches (18cm)

*Identification:* The Dunlin can be distinguished from the Stints by its larger size and by its longer bill which is slightly down-curved. It is invariably seen feeding frantically with bill in and out of the sand at great speed. In summer there is a black patch on the belly. In flight a short, faint wing bar is visible. The tail is dark grey and there is a black bar which runs through the white rump and grey tail.

*Habitat:* Coastal areas and by inland water.

*Status in Central Arabia:* Passage migrant.

*Status in Arabian Peninsula:* Winter visitor and passage migrant to most coastal areas though more common in the east than the west.

Left: *This Little Stint, photographed in January, shows many of the characteristics necessary to identify the species. Note the black legs, and straight black bill.*

## KNOT
*Calidris canutus*
10 inches (25cm)

*Identification:* In winter plumage (which is the only form in which it can be seen in the area) this stocky-looking wader is dark brownish-grey above with a scaly pattern on the wings which have pale grey edges. The underparts are white with a very faint grey band running round the breast. There is a white stripe above the eye and white round the base of the black bill. The eyes are black and appear very large, due to the black smudge immediately in front of them and there is a pale fawn patch behind the eye. The legs are yellowish-brown. In flight the wings are a medium grey with a paler bar; the tail is faintly barred.

*Habitat:* Generally on the coast but occasionally will visit inland water edges and they can be seen wading in shallow water with their bills and faces deep down in the water.

*Status in Central Arabia:* Rare passage migrant. A flock of 10 were observed on one occasion in September (and gone the next day), a surprise sighting since their normal migratory route is not over this area.

*Status in Arabian Peninsula:* Uncommon passage migrant in the east and southeast.

Above: *A Dunlin in winter plumage. Compare the long, slightly down-curved bill with the Little Stint's.*

Centre right: *The Knot.*

## BROAD-BILLED SANDPIPER
*Limicola falcinellus*
7 inches (18cm)

*Identification:* This wader appears out of proportion with its shortish legs, relatively heavy-looking body with a thick neck and a bill that is very broad at the base and slightly down-curved at the tip. In breeding plumage the upperparts are dark with two cream-

*Allied Species*
## TEMMINCK'S STINT (*Calidris temminckii*) is an uncommon winter visitor and passage migrant to most parts of the peninsula. It is very similar to the Little Stint but distinguished from it by a more definite band across the breast and by paler, more greenish, legs. When flushed from cover it flies directly up into the air unlike the Little Stint.

## COMMON SANDPIPER
*Tringa hypoleucos*
7¾ inches (20cm)

*Identification:* This medium-sized wader is less streaked and mottled on the upperparts than other sandpipers; the head, mantle and wings are an almost matt olive-brown and there is a low lightly streaked brown bib. The underparts are white and continue up

coloured bars on each side of the back; the very distinct white eyestripe forks very clearly behind the eye. The underparts are white with contrasting brown streaking on the breast. In winter the upperparts are not so dark and the cream bars are not present; the distinctive fork of the eyestripe is not so clear but the stripe broadens behind the eye; a distinct darkening of the wing at the carpal joint is noticeable when the bird is on the ground.

*Habitat:* Mud-flats and lagoons.

*Status in Central Arabia:* Uncommon passage migrant.

*Status in Arabian Peninsula:* Winter visitor and passage migrant to most parts of the peninsula.

Above left: *The Broad-billed Sandpiper also has a slightly down-curved bill but has different markings.*
Above right: *Common Sandpiper.*

The **SANDERLING** (*Calidris alba*) is a passage migrant and winter visitor to most parts of the peninsula. Larger than the Dunlin, it is more rufous in summer and much whiter in winter when it can be distinguished by black spots on the shoulder. In flight there is a more prominent white wing bar and white at the sides of the black rump.

The larger **CURLEW SANDPIPER** (*Calidris ferruginea*) (7½ inches/19cm) can be identified in both plumages by its long black down-curved bill, its prominent white rump and (in breeding season) by its dark rufous plumage. In September and October most of the birds still have rufous remaining on the breast and upper belly. They are fairly common passage migrants over most of the peninsula east of, and including, Riyadh.

to the shoulder to make an inverted 'V' between wing and bib. There is a pale fawn stripe through the eye; the bill is brownish with black at the tip and the legs are yellowish-grey. On the ground it bobs its head and tail. In flight there is a broad white wing bar and, as an aid to identification, the birds have an unusual habit of dropping the tips of their wings on the downbeat.

*Habitat:* Beside salt or fresh water.

*Status in Central Arabia:* Passage migrant.

*Status in Arabian Peninsula:* Passage migrant and winter visitor to almost all parts of the peninsula.

Below: *A Terek Sandpiper showing the slightly up-curved bill.*

# TEREK SANDPIPER
*Tringa cinereus*
9 inches (23cm)

*Identification:* This slightly larger sandpiper is grey-brown above with pale brown streaks on nape and shoulder. Underparts are white, the legs yellowish-grey and the long gently up-curved bill makes it one of the easier birds to identify. No wing bar shows in flight. On the ground this bird also bobs its head and tail and will run very fast through shallow water with its head lowered.

*Habitat:* Coastal areas and beside inland water and on marshy ground.

*Status in Central Arabia:* Spring migrant, a few birds remaining during summer months although there has been no evidence recorded of breeding.

*Status in Arabian Peninsula:* Passage migrant and winter visitor to most parts of the peninsula.

# WOOD SANDPIPER
*Tringa glareola*
8 inches (20cm)

*Identification:* The mantle and wings are a dark olive-brown, liberally spotted with white. There is brown streaking down the creamish breast, a black eyestripe with a creamy one above and black bars across the white tail. The legs are yellowish-grey and the bill black. In flight there is no wing bar, the legs protrude very slightly and a white rump above the barred tail is conspicuous.

*Habitat:* Beside fresh water.

*Status in Central Arabia:* Common winter visitor with a few birds remaining throughout the year.

*Status in Arabian Peninsula:* Passage migrant and winter visitor to most areas where there is suitable habitat.

Left: *A Wood Sandpiper showing the perfection of its camouflage.*

## GREEN SANDPIPER
*Tringa ochropus*
9 inches (23cm)

*Identification:* The Green Sandpiper is dark blackish brown above with scarcely discernable light tips to the feathers. The throat is unstreaked, the breast is streaked dark brown with heavier streaking to the sides and there is a dark eyestripe with a paler one above. The legs are dark. It is most easy to identify in flight when the very dark wings and mantle contrast markedly with the extensive pure white rump. It is the most frustrating of birds – it is always the first of any group of waders to take alarm and its loud and agitated 'weeter-weet' cries as it climbs swiftly into the air before flying off, ensure that all other waders nearby follow suit.

*Habitat:* Inland lagoons, lakes and water-filled wadis.

*Status in Central Arabia:* Appears to be resident – observed throughout the year in fair numbers.

*Status in Arabian Peninsula:* Winter visitor and passage migrant to most parts of the peninsula.

Below: *The Green Sandpiper with white rump, dark tail and back resembles, in flight, a large House Martin.*

Below: *This Redshank clearly shows the reason for its name.*

## GREENSHANK
*Tringa nebularia*
12 inches (30.5cm)

*Identification:* One of the largest of the Tringa family, this bird is a very pale grey with slightly darker blue-grey wings; it has a white throat, lightly striped pale grey breast and a faint white eyestripe above the beady black eye and a long, dark, very slightly up-curved bill. The legs are long and dark greenish-grey. In flight the white rump extends in a clearly marked inverted 'V' half way up the back and there is no wing bar.

*Habitat:* Beside permanent water.

*Status in Central Arabia:* Passage migrant.

*Status in Arabian Peninsula:* Passage migrant and winter visitor to Hejaz, the northwest, Eastern Province, Oman and UAE.

Below: *The Greenshank.*

## REDSHANK
*Tringa totanus*
11 inches (28cm)

*Identification:* The Redshank is a brownish bird with darker spots on mantle and wings; the underparts are paler with brown streaks on the breast. The legs and the thin straight bill are red. It is the only wader to show a broad white hind wing; the white rump extends into a short inverted 'V'.

*Habitat:* By coastal or inland water.

yellow or black and bills vary in the same way. The feathers of the back of the Ruff or Reeve are edged with pale buff which gives the bird a scaly appearance which helps to distinguish it from the Redshank. However, a certain way to distinguish one from the other on the ground is by size. The Ruff is much bigger and Reeves are heavier-loooking with thicker necks than the more delicate Redshank. (In a group of three or four similar birds the biggest and heaviest one will be a Ruff, the others Reeves.) In flight separation is easier as there is a white wing bar instead of the Redshank's white edge to the rear portion of the wing.

*Habitat:* Beside salt or fresh water.

*Status in Central Arabia:* Commonly seen in all months of the year with peaks in April and September/October.

*Status in Arabian Peninsula:* Passage migrant and winter visitor to most parts of the peninsula.

*Allied Species*
The **MARSH SANDPIPER** (*Tringa stagnatilis*) is a passage migrant and winter visitor to most parts of the peninsula where there is permanent water. It is a slim and very graceful wader with a pattern of dark diamonds on both its fawn mantle and its wings and with dark spots on the breast and flanks. The head is small and rounded, the bill is long and very thin, there is a pale stripe just above the eye and the long legs are pale greenish-grey. There is no wing bar and the white rump runs up the back into a long narrow inverted 'V'.

The **SPOTTED REDSHANK**
(*Tringa erythropus*) is a passage migrant and winter visitor to most parts of the peninsula. In breeding plumage it is dark sooty black speckled with white on its mantle and wings. In winter it can be separated from the Redshank by its darker wings, its lack of streaks on its breast and (in flight) by its lack of white hind wing.

*Status in Central Arabia:* Uncommon passage migrant.

*Status in Arabian Peninsula:* Passage migrant to almost all parts of the peninsula.

Above: *The Ruff in winter plumage. This bird clearly shows the scaly appearance of its back that is diagnostic in its identification. This appearance is produced by the pale tips of the feathers contrasting with the darker surround.*

**RUFF & REEVE**
*Philomachus pugnax*
Ruff $11\frac{1}{2}$ inches (29cm)
Reeve 9 inches (23cm)

*Identification:* In non-breeding plumage (they only breed in the northern parts of Europe) the male (Ruff) and the female (Reeve) are hard to distinguish from Redshanks when on the ground. Both are brown birds with darker spots on wing and mantle and both have long legs and bills, always red in Redshanks but variable in colour in Ruffs and Reeves. Legs can be red,

## SNIPE
*Gallinago gallinago*
10½ inches (26cm)

*Identification:* The Snipe is one of a handful of birds that possesses its own collective noun – a group of snipe is called a 'wisp'. This brown wader is distinguished from all others (apart from other snipes) by its really very long and straight bill and by the six black stripes running along the head. The wings and mantle are darkly streaked, the throat and breast are also streaked black on brown. The belly and underparts are white. The legs are short and dark. They are very often seen in pairs and, as they squat in a sheltered corner, with their long bills seeming too heavy to hold up, they seem a real 'Derby and Joan' couple. When flushed they emit a loud, harsh, swiftly repeated 'creek, creek, creek' and fly off with a zig-zag flight.

*Habitat:* Beside banks at waters edge where their camouflage is near perfect. Occasionally seen on rocks or branches in shallow water.

*Status in Central Arabia:* Winter visitor – observed in most months of the year apart from midsummer.

*Status in Arabian Peninsula:* Passage migrant and winter visitor to Eastern Province, the northwest and Oman.

## CURLEW
*Numenius arquata*
21 inches (53cm)

*Identification:* This solitary bird has an almost unbelievably long, down-curved bill. Its plumage is brown with black 'arrowheads' on mantle and wings and dark streaks around the neck and on the breast. The tail is brown with black bars. In flight the upper side is brown, darker at the tips of the wings and a white rump is conspicuous; from below the bird is much paler. The slightly protruding legs and the very long bill give it a distinctly weird appearance as it rather majestically sails by. Its loud cry of 'kurrrl-eee' is distinctive.

*Habitat:* Coastal areas.

*Status in Arabian Peninsula:* Passage migrant and winter visitor to most coastal areas.

Top: *The massive bill of the Snipe enables it to probe deep into the mud in search of the small animals on which it feeds. The tip of the bill is highly sensitive and flexible thus allowing it to feel movements in the sand.*
Above: *A Curlew in flight showing the long down-curved bill.*

## WHIMBREL
*Numenius phaeopus*
16 inches (41cm)

*Identification:* The Whimbrel is much smaller than the Curlew and has a less disproportionately long bill. The colouring is very similar but at close quarters two dark stripes on the top of the head are noticeable above a pale eyestripe.

*Habitat:* Coastal areas.

*Status in Arabian Peninsula:* Passage migrant and winter visitor to the Gulf Coast and Oman.

## CREAM-COLOURED COURSER
*Cursorius cursor*
9 inches (23cm)

*Identification:* The Cream-Coloured Courser is a pale sand-coloured bird with black at the edge of the folded

## COLLARED PRATINCOLE
*Glareola pratincola*
10 inches (25cm)

*Identification:* These birds, with their long, angled, narrow and sharply pointed wings, together with a deeply forked tail, look very similar to swallows when in flight. On the ground, by the water's edge, its unusual shape makes it hard to mistake for any other bird. It has a round head, a short neck, a very short bill and stands squarely on its stout black legs. The plumage is brown above and on the breast and, on adult birds, there is a conspicuous cream throat bordered with black. Juveniles are without the pure cream throat and their overall brown plumage is beautifully vermiculated with black and white. In flight a white rump is conspicuous as is the black at the tip of the forked tail. The coverts on the underwing are a rusty-red but this is only visible at extremely close quarters – it is particularly noticeable when the bird raises its wings prior to take-off.

*Habitat:* Generally by water.

*Status in Central Arabia:* Short-term passage migrants in fairly large numbers.

*Status in Arabian Peninsula:* Passage migrant.

The **STONE CURLEW** (*Burhinus oedicnemus*) is an uncommon visitor observed on one occasion by the author in the stony desert west of Riyadh and reported occasionally in other parts of the peninsula. Its colouring is sandy-brown with black at the edge of the folded wing and there is a white wing bar. It merges perfectly into its background and its habit of 'freezing' when approached makes it extremely hard to spot. It will get up almost at the walker's feet and it is then that the boldly patterned black, white and brown of the wing makes its identification certain.

Top right: *Immature Collared Pratincole.*
Above: *The Whimbrel. Compare the bill length with that of the Curlew opposite.*

wing. There is a black stripe running behind the eye with a white one above; the bill is short and down-curved and the legs are long and very pale. The bird merges perfectly into a sandy background. In flight it is more distinctive as the dark tips to the upper wings and the completely black underwing are in marked contrast to the pale creamy colour of the rest of the body. Its most characteristic feature is its behaviour on the ground – it runs at great speed with the body almost horizontal and, when it stops, squats back on its haunches and digs its bill in and out of the sand at great speed.

*Habitat:* Open sand or stone desert.

*Status in Central Arabia:* Resident breeding in small numbers.

*Status in Arabian Peninsula:* Resident breeding in Eastern Province and Oman.

Above: *Rock Dove.*

David Dinnell

Above: *Collared Dove.*

These large land birds are generally coloured in shades of grey, brown and blue-green. Sexes are alike apart from the Namaqua. Their flight is vigorous, the sound of their wingbeats being easily heard and they can generally be recognised by frequent positioning of the wings into a deepish 'V'.

## ROCK DOVE
*Columba livia*
13 inches (33cm)

*Identification:* These birds are the ancestors of the domestic pigeon; the feral pigeons that can be seen in many

*Habitat:* Most areas, coastal and inland, where there are cliffs but they are also found in the middle of open desert where they will nest inside a well.

*Status throughout Arabian Peninsula:* Resident breeding in most areas.

## COLLARED DOVE
*Streptopelis decaocto*
12½ inches (32cm)

*Identification:* The Collared Dove is a greyish-brown bird with a pinkish-grey breast and black tips to pale grey wings; there is a black half-collar on the nape with a faint white band above. In flight the underwing shows medium grey on the flight feathers and off-white on the coverts. The underside of the tail is black at the base and broadly tipped white; the upperside is grey, tipped white on the outer feathers. The call is a persistent triple 'coo-*cooo*-cuh'. Although they are common they are extremely wary of humans and very difficult to approach.

*Habitat:* Commonly seen in towns, villages and near cultivation.

*Status throughout Arabian Peninsula:* Resident breeding in all parts, except in Hejaz and Asir where they are seldom seen.

*Laughing or Palm Dove.*

Above: *Turtle Dove.*

towns throughout the world are their descendants as are the spectacularly coloured 'falling' pigeons seen in various parts of this peninsula.

The Rock Dove is grey-blue in colour with paler grey wings, each marked with a pair of black crescent bars. The nape is greenish-blue and there is a purplish collar. There is a black tip to the grey tail. In most areas they have a white rump but Rock Doves in Arabia do not generally have one.

## PALM/LAUGHING DOVE
*Streptopelis senegalensis*
10¼ inches (26cm)

*Identification:* The Palm Dove is a pinkish-grey dove with blue wings tipped with black. The rather large area of black spots on the pink breast is distinctive. In flight the wings show blue-grey in front and black at the rear; the black tail is tipped with white. The call is a variable series of 'coos' delivered in ascending and descending notes.

*Habitat:* Towns, villages and near cultivation.

*Status throughout Arabian Peninsula:* Resident breeding in all parts of the peninsula except for the centre where it is, surprisingly, not known.

## TURTLE DOVE
*Streptopelis turtur*
11 inches (27cm)

*Identification:* This grey-headed, pink-breasted dove has dark brownish-chestnut speckled wings. Adult birds have a small white patch, covered with thin black stripes, on each side of the neck. In flight the underwing is uniformly medium grey and the black tail is narrowly edged with white. Immature birds are greyer and are without the neck patches. There is also a much paler, more sandy-coloured form with the same tail pattern as the 'normal' one.

*Habitat:* Desert country with acacia and beside cultivation.

*Status in Central Arabia:* Probably resident breeding. Observed in most months of the year, though in greater numbers during the summer.

*Status in Arabian Peninsula:* Summer visitor to most areas.

## PINK-BREASTED DOVE
*Streptopelia lugens*
11 inches (27cm)

*Identification:* In flight this bird appears a soft charcoal-grey all over, slightly paler below and a little darker on head and tail. The tail feathers each have a small white spot almost at the tip, and when the tail is fanned these appear as a very thin white line. At rest the mantle shows dark grey, the grey wing feathers are tipped with orange, the face and throat are almost white and there is a broad dark grey patch on each side of the neck. The belly is pinkish-grey and there is a distinct pink tinge on the upper breast. The eye is red and the bill black.

*Habitat:* Well-wooded wadis.

*Status in Arabian Peninsula:* Not known. About seven or eight were observed by the author in a wadi near Abha in October and were common on the summit of Jebel Soodah in April.

Left: *Pink-breasted Dove.*

# NAMAQUA DOVE
*Oena capensis*
11 inches (27cm)

*Identification:* The Namaqua is a beautiful and very unusual-looking dove. Disregarding its five inches of tail it is remarkably small and it is the only long-tailed dove of the area. The male has a soft grey back, darkening at the tail, which is black; the underparts are white and he has an unmistakable black face and throat; the bill is short and bright red. The female is the same as her mate except that she lacks the black face and throat – she is, as a consequence, more delicate-looking. In flight the birds are almost breathtakingly lovely – the pure white underparts contrast vividly with the black tail and the deep crimson of the underwing against the sun. Fledglings are spotted black and white and juveniles are an unlikely mixture of grey, white and chestnut. The call is a weak 'kwoo-cuh' and it is sometimes hard to trace the source of the sound.

*Habitat:* Palm groves.

*Status in Central Arabia:* Resident, breeding in a few localised areas though they would appear to be spreading fairly rapidly.

*Status in Arabian Peninsula:* Present in Hejaz, Eastern Province and Kuwait in growing numbers.

Below: *Female Namaqua Dove.*

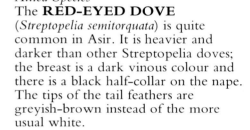

*Allied Species*
## The RED-EYED DOVE
(*Streptopelia semitorquata*) is quite common in Asir. It is heavier and darker than other Streptopelia doves; the breast is a dark vinous colour and there is a black half-collar on the nape. The tips of the tail feathers are greyish-brown instead of the more usual white.

## BRUCE'S GREEN PIGEON
(*Treron waalia*) is also commonly found in well-wooded areas in Asir and Oman. The upperparts are apple-green apart from soft grey at the neck; the breast and belly are bright yellow and the legs are red.

Right: *Juvenile Namaqua Dove.*

Above: *Male Namaqua Dove.*

These are the birds of brilliant plumage – bright greens, blues, purples and yellows – the birds commonly associated with warmth and sun.

## KINGFISHER
*Alcedo atthis*
6½ inches (16.5cm)

*Identification:* Just a glimpse of this brilliantly coloured bird as it flashes by over running water is a breath-taking sight. The upperparts are bright turquoise blue; the feathers on the crown and wings are tipped with black. Underparts are rich, rosy chestnut with white at the throat. The stout bill is a dark horn colour. They are generally seen in pairs. During the winter months the underparts are very much paler.

*Habitat:* Mainly by fresh running water with bushes by the water's edge, but also by salt water.

*Status in Central Arabia:* No confirmed sighting in the area though on two occasions, both in September, there was an almost unmistakable flash of blue at the Mansouriyah lakes, so perhaps they are rare passage migrants.

*Status in Arabian Peninsula:* Resident breeding in Bahrain and Asir. Winter visitor to Eastern Province and the Gulf Coast.

Right: *European Kingfisher watching for fish.*

Above: *The green wing of this Kingfisher suggests that it is a young bird.*

Below: *A pair of Pied Kingfishers.*

## PIED KINGFISHER
*Ceryle rudis*
10 inches (25cm)

*Identification:* This totally black and white bird has a stout black bill and a rather flattened black crest. The male has two black bars across the white breast and the female has just one. When fishing they hover above the water with frantically beating wings and then plummet into the water.

*Habitat:* Frequents both salt and fresh water but is more generally seen near the latter.

*Status in Arabian Peninsula:* Probably a winter visitor to a few parts of the western Gulf. A pair were observed by the author in Bahrain in December/January.

*Allied Specie*
The **GREY-HEADED KINGFISHER** (*Halcyon leucocephala*) is found in Hejaz and Asir. It has a red bill, grey head, chestnut underparts and a blue tail; the mantle and wing coverts are black and the flight feathers blue.

# Bee-eaters (Meropidae)

Bee-Eaters are brightly coloured insect-eating birds with long tails and slightly down-curved bills. The underwing is, in all cases, chestnut in colour though the shade varies according to specie. Sexes are alike. They are gregarious and vocal. Having caught their prey by a swift sortie into the air they will return to their perch in order to kill and then eat it.

face above and below a black eyestripe. There is a black quarter collar below the throat. Even in breeding season the central tail feathers protrude only a little. In winter and during the hottest part of the year the bird becomes duller, more brownish on its neck and mantle and there is slightly less blue about the face. In flight the entire underwing is an almost transparent pale chestnut. A soft insistent 'pree, pree, pree' tells of their presence overhead.

*Habitat:* Almost anywhere where there is an acacia tree. They perch on low

Below: *In common with other Bee-eaters the Little Green Bee-eater is a very handsome bird.*

## LITTLE GREEN BEE-EATER
*Merops orientalis najdanus*
8 inches (21cm)

*Identification:* This Little Green, which is resident in Arabia, is a separate race to the one illustrated in most bird books. For most of the year it is a beautiful bright green bird with a touch of russet on the neck and mantle and with a lot of vivid blue on the

branches, low banks and on low barbed wire.

*Status in Central Arabia:* Resident breeding. Observed throughout the year.

*Status in Arabian Peninsula:* Resident breeding in Hejaz, the northwest, UAE and Oman. Passage migrant in Eastern Province and the Gulf Coast.

## EUROPEAN BEE-EATER
*Merops apiaster*
11 inches (28cm)

*Identification:* The European Bee-Eater is a striking multi-coloured bird with dark chestnut head, nape and mantle, a very prominent yellow throat and turquoise underparts. The central tail feathers protrude slightly from the dark blue-green tail. In flight the bird can be identified by the very pale chestnut underwing edged with black and by the very prominent yellow throat. The cry is a continuous loud, liquid 'peeu-peeu-peeu'.

*Habitat:* Wadis, palm groves and by permanent water. They fly and perch at a higher level than the Little Greens.

*Status in Central Arabia:* Passage migrant.

*Status in Arabian Peninsula:* Summer visitor and passage migrant to the southeast. Passage migrant to Hejaz and the northwest.

*Below: A European Bee-eater rests after a bee-catching session in the fall.*
*Right: Blue-cheeked Bee-eater.*

## BLUE-CHEEKED BEE-EATER
*Merops superciliosus*
12 inches (31cm)

*Identification:* In spite of its name this bird has less blue on its face than the Little Green. It has a dark green plumage (brighter during the spring migration), a bit of blue above and below a broad black eyestripe and a dull orange throat. In flight the underwing is dark chestnut, almost crimson in bright sunlight. The long central tail feathers are not evident during the periods the bird migrates through Arabia. The call resembles a soft, short police whistle.

*Habitat:* By permanent water. Perches on high trees and wires from which it swoops low over the water to catch its prey.

*Status throughout Peninsula:* Passage migrant to Hejaz, the centre, the northwest, Eastern Province and Oman. Reported to breed in UAE.

*Allied Specie*
The **WHITE-THROATED BEE-EATER** (*Aerops albicollis*) has been recorded in the Hejaz on the Jeddah-Mecca Road. This bird can be identified by its paler colouring, white throat with a prominent black band below, cinnamon-coloured underwing and long tail streamers.

## INDIAN ROLLER
*Coracias benghalensis*
13 inches (33cm)

*Identification:* Perched on a telephone wire, lamp-post or treetop this bird looks dun-coloured and rather ordinary. Close up, however, he becomes more interesting; there is a bright blue crown, bright blue on the edge of the folded wing, a bright blue belly and blue on the outer tail feathers. The pale buff rather ruffled feathers on the throat and breast are tipped with black and white, the eyes and the stout bill are black and the legs reddish. When the bird takes off he is transformed into a brilliant blue with the brown colour scarcely noticeable; the large broad wings are mainly bright sky blue, tipped and edged with purplish-black. In early spring the male can commonly be seen performing aerial courtship displays – steep climbs into the air followed by a rolling descent. These aerobatics, which attract attention in the breeding season, are performed by all the rollers and have given them their name. It feeds on large insects.

Top: *Indian Roller.*
Above: *European Roller.*

*Habitat:* Near cultivation, wooded areas, gardens etc.

*Status in Arabian Peninsula:* Resident breeding in UAE and probably in Oman. Passage migrant or winter visitor elsewhere in eastern parts of the peninsula.

## EUROPEAN ROLLER
*Coracias garrulus*
12 inches (31cm)

*Identification:* This bird has the same general appearance and habits as the Indian but when perched he is much more striking as only his mantle is chestnut brown; the rest of his body is sky blue with blue-black at the edge of the folded wing. On take-off he is marginally less spectacular, perhaps because there is a less marked transformation. The forewing is bright blue and the tips and rear edges are almost black. The juvenile lacks the blue head.

*Habitat:* Much the same as above but more often found in proximity to water.

*Status in Central Arabia:* Uncommon passage migrant. Sadly they are a popular target for the gun and roller feathers can occasionally be found among spent cartridge cases.

*Status in Arabian Peninsula:* Passage migrant to most parts of the peninsula.

Above: *Abyssinian Roller.*

Betty Vincett

## ABYSSINIAN ROLLER
*Coracias abyssinicus*
16 inches (41cm)

*Identification:* The Abyssinian is very similar to the European but the colours are all more vivid and the contrast between colours more marked. The outer tail feathers are elongated to form long streamers.

*Habitat:* Well-wooded wadis.

*Status in Arabian Peninsula:* Passage migrant to Asir. One or two have also been reported around Harad to the east of Riyadh.

*Allied Specie*
The **LILAC-BREASTED ROLLER** (*Coracias caudata*) has been reliably reported on a few occasions around Jeddah. It is pale blue on its belly and crown, lilac on its throat and breast, fawn on the mantle and has blue wings. The outer tail feathers protrude an inch or two.

## HOOPOE
*Upupa epops*
11 inches (28cm)

*Identification:* This is the classic 'extraordinary-looking bird we saw . . .' that, once identified, can never be mistaken for anything else. The head, neck and breast are cinnamon; the rounded wings and mantle are broadly striped black and white; the tail is black with two white bars across the base; the black bill is long and down-curved and there is a prominent black and white tipped cinnamon crest which is sometimes folded down to

protrude from the back of the head and sometimes fanned to cover the whole top of the head. They are generally solitary though during migration they may be seen in large numbers. The call is a far-carrying 'hoo-hoo-hoo'.

*Habitat:* Almost anywhere. Generally on the ground pecking for small insects.

*Status in Central Arabia:* Resident breeding in small numbers; summer visitor in greater numbers.

*Status in Arabian Peninsula:* Resident breeding in Hejaz, the northwest and Bahrain; passage migrant to most other areas.

The **GREY HORNBILL** (*Tockus nasutus*) is fairly common in the extreme south of Asir. It is brownish-grey all over except for the breast and belly which are off-white. The heavy, curved bill is black in the male and reddish brown in the female.

Below left: *A Hoopoe with the crest up.*
Below right: *The Hoopoe.*

## RING-NECKED PARAKEET
*Psittacula krameri*
16 inches (41cm)

*Identification:* This is the only member of the parrot family in the area – in all probability they were originally escaped cage birds which have bred and multiplied. Both sexes are bright emerald green with long tails (almost twice the length of their bodies) and short, hooked red bills. The male (only) has a black band at the throat and a pink one round the back of his neck. They are always seen in flocks of varying size. The call, which is most often uttered in flight, is an oft-repeated monosyllabic screech.

*Habitat:* Gardens, palm groves, tree-lined streets. Particularly fond of sunflower seeds.

*Status in Central Arabia:* Not certain but probably a winter visitor. Believed to be more abundant in wetter years.

*Status in Arabian Peninsula:* Breeds in Bahrain, UAE and probably in Eastern Province.

75

# 6 Birds of Sombre Plumage

*Yellow-vented Bulbuls*, Pycnonotus xanthopygos

Birds from many different families are included in this broad group. All have, basically, brown, black or grey plumage though a few have patches of brighter colour.

## WRYNECK
*Jynx torquilla*
$6\frac{1}{2}$ inches (16.5cm)

*Identification:* This bird is a member of the Woodpecker family and has its characteristic feet – two claws in front and two behind. It is a strange-looking bird, grey-brown in colour with short horizontal streaks covering the palish throat, breast and belly. The upperparts are darker and there are two very pronounced unstreaked pale grey bars, one on either side of the head above the eye and one running down the shoulder above the wing. The tail is long and striped horizontally with black and two shades of grey. It frequently flies to the ground to find ants which are a favourite food. The flight is low and very direct, quite unlike the bounding flight of other woodpeckers.

*Habitat:* Palm groves.

*Status in Central Arabia:* Passage migrant.

*Status in Arabian Peninsula:* Passage migrant in Hejaz, Asir, the northwest and Eastern Province.

*Allied Specie*
## The **ARABIAN WOODPECKER**
(*Picoides dorae*) is present in well-treed wadis in Asir and Hejaz. It is dull brown in colour with black wings spotted white. There is a dull red patch on the belly but this is hardly noticeable in the field, and the male has a crimson patch on the back of his head, which is also hard to spot. The black tail has white spots on the outer feathers, the legs are black and the medium length black bill is very pointed. They perch astride a branch in an almost horizontal posture.

Above: *Wryneck.*

Below: *Arabian Sand Partridge.*

## ARABIAN SAND PARTRIDGE
*Ammoperdix heyi*
$9\frac{1}{2}$ inches (24cm)

*Identification:* These birds are extremely shy and difficult to approach. Experience must have taught them that the appearance of the human race bodes them no good and, as a result, they can generally be seen beating a hasty retreat up the sides of a steep wadi or escarpment. If they are taken by surprise (and the observer is far too frequently as surprised as they are) they will take off with the usual partridge 'whirr' of wings and fly off, low, to a safer spot. They are sandy-brown in colour, plump-looking and have a very short tail. The male is strongly barred with chestnut, black and white on the flanks and has a prominent white spot behind the eye. The female is paler, finely vermiculated all over and lacks the white eye spot.

*Habitat:* Deep rocky wadis and beside escarpments.

*Status in Central Arabia:* Resident breeding.

*Status in Arabian Peninsula:* Breeds in the UAE mountains and in Asir.

## TUFTED GUINEAFOWL
*Numida meleagris*
25 inches (62cm)

*Identification:* The mantle, wings, tail, breast and belly of this large game-bird are blue-grey and covered in white spots. The broad hooked bill, wattle and bony crest are red; the sides of the face are unfeathered and whitish.

*Habitat:* Well vegetated areas beside permanent water.

*Status in Arabian Peninsula:* Resident in Asir but extremely localised.

*Allied Species*
The **QUAIL** (*Coturnix coturnix*) is resident in the high ground of Asir and Hejaz and is a passage migrant to a few areas around the Gulf Coast. It is reddish-brown above with black markings on its mantle and wings and white stripes running down the flanks; the breast is brownish and the belly pale fawn. The male has a black throat and a white half-collar on the lower neck.

## The **GREY FRANCOLIN**
(*Francolinus pondicerianus*) breeds in UAE and Oman. It is greyish-brown all over, heavily vermiculated black and white above but fainter below. The legs are reddish.

Above: *Tufted Guineafowl on the alert.*

## CUCKOO
*Cuculus canorus*
13 inches (33cm)

*Identification:* This grey (or occasionally rufous) bird in flight can be mistaken for a falcon due to the narrow, pointed wings and long tail which sometimes appears forked. White spots on the dark grey tail are arranged in horizontal lines and are conspicuous in flight and when perched. Upperparts of the adult male are soft grey and the off-white underparts (below the grey throat and upper breast) are finely barred black. Females and juveniles are generally barred all over and juveniles can be heavily spotted white on the dark grey wings. The bill is short, down-curved and horn-coloured with a yellow gape, particularly noticeable in immature birds. The cuckoo perches almost horizontally along a branch or palm-frond with wings drooping on either side as if to keep its balance. The mystery surrounding the migratory instinct of birds is heightened in this bird. The female lays her eggs in the nests of other birds and the young cuckoo, therefore, grows up away from its mother and, in spite of this, manages to find its way from Europe to Africa. All the birds observed by the author, taking temporary refuge in date-laden palm groves, have been juveniles.

*Habitat:* Palm groves.

*Status in Central Arabia:* Passage migrant in small numbers.

*Status in Arabian Peninsula:* Uncommon passage migrant to most parts of the peninsula.

*Allied Specie*
The **GREAT-SPOTTED CUCKOO** (*Clamator glandarius*) has occasionally been seen in central Arabia and in Eastern Province. It is dark grey above with white spots on the wings, cream below and has an unmistakable pale grey crest and a red eye.

The **SWIFT** (*Apus apus*) is a passage migrant over almost all parts of the peninsula. This totally aerial bird covers thousands of miles in spring and again in autumn and is known from Scandinavia to southern Africa. It is dark all over apart from a faint lightening on the throat. The wings are narrow and scythe-like and the tail fairly short and deeply cleft.

The **PALLID SWIFT** (*Apus pallidus*) is a migrant breeder in one or two isolated rocky areas and also a passage migrant in larger numbers. It is difficult to separate the two species but the Pallid is slightly more brown than black and has a more pronounced lightening at the throat.

## YELLOW-VENTED BULBUL
*Pycnonotus xanthopygos*
$7\frac{1}{2}$ inches (19cm)

*Identification:* This Bulbul is a dark brownish-grey above with a 'square' black head and throat, a long dark grey tail, paler underparts and yellow undertail coverts. There is a conspicuous white circle round the black eye. They are gregarious birds and follow one another from tree to tree informing the observer of their presence by their rich, almost, liquid, song often uttered in flight. When perched they will converse with one another with a scolding rattle.

*Habitat:* Gardens, palm groves, bushes in remote wadis. One of the most widespread birds of the area.

*Status in Central Arabia:* Very common. Resident breeding.

*Status in Arabian Peninsula:* Resident breeding in most parts west of the central region and in the UAE mountains and Oman.

Opposite: *An immature Cuckoo photographed in September while it was on passage to Africa, probably having already flown two thousand miles from northern Europe.*

Right: *Yellow-vented Bulbul. This common species is quite a pleasant songster.*

## WHITE-EARED BULBUL
*Pycnonotus leucogenys*
7 inches (18cm)

*Identification:* The White-Eared Bulbul is similar to the Yellow-Vented but with a blacker and less square head and with prominent white cheek patches below the eye. The undertail coverts are orange-yellow and there are white spots at the tip of the black tail. This bulbul makes more play with its tail, flicking it up high above the head and wagging it from side to side. More often seen in pairs than in groups and they appear to have confidential talks with each other.

Their song is a softer and quieter 'Oo-toodle-oo'.

*Habitat:* As above.

*Status in Arabian Peninsula:* The two species never seem to overlap; the White-Eared is a resident breeder in most parts of the peninsula where the Yellow-Vented is absent. Breeds in Eastern Province and in Bahrain.

Right: *The White-eared Bulbul also has a yellow vent, but has white cheek patches unlike the yellow-vented.*

## ARABIAN BABBLER
*Turdoides squamiceps*
10 inches (26.5cm)

*Identification:* This medium large grey-brown bird has a long, graduated, grey tail with which it makes much play, flicking it up and down and from side to side. There is a scaly effect on the head, face, nape and upper breast and also, to a lesser extent, on the throat which is not as white as generally depicted. The black bill is down-curved and there is a deep yellow line extending from the base of the bill to a point below the eye; this line is not noticeable except at extremely close quarters. Usually the birds are seen in groups of from six to 10 and their curious squeaky cries are more reminiscent of a collection of mice than a flock of birds. When disturbed they will leave the tree one by one, following each other with a jerky, laboured flight ending in a long glide on stretched wings and spread tail as they approach their next port of call. Towards dusk they will perform curious fluttering 'dances', rising into the air and seeming to shake themselves.

*Habitat:* Palm groves or other well-treed areas.

*Status in Central Arabia:* Resident breeding in fairly small numbers. Numbers increase during the summer months.

*Status in Arabian Peninsula:* Resident breeding in Hejaz, Eastern Province, Oman and UAE.

## SWALLOW
*Hirundo rustica*
7½ inches (19cm)

*Identification:* Probably the best known of all birds, the Swallow is welcomed in both hemispheres as the harbinger of summer. The plumage is deep blue-black above and buff below; there is a crimson face and throat which ends in a black band. When flying high the crimson is not distinguishable and the whole head appears black. Their tails

Above: *Immature Swallow. Note the short tail feathers.*

Above: *Adult Swallow showing long tail streamers.*

Opposite: *Arabian Babbler. This bird has a complex social structure consisting of both family groups and unmated 'bachelor' groups.*

Below: *Sand Martins on migration to Africa.*

*Habitat:* Over towns and open countryside. Large numbers will congregate over areas of permanent water and they will often roost on low branches or on barbed wire in such vicinities.

distinguishable from the Swallow by its reddish fawn rump and by the red band on the nape; there is no black band on the breast and no white spots on the tail. It is reported to breed in Hejaz and is a passage migrant to most other areas.

## SAND MARTIN
*Riparia riparia*
$4\frac{3}{4}$ inches (12cm)

*Identification:* The Sand Martin is a very small bird with a distinctive brown breast band across his otherwise white underparts. Wings, short cleft tail and all upperparts are dark brown.

*Habitat:* Over permanent water.

*Status in Arabian Peninsula:* Passage migrant to Hejaz, the centre, the northwest and Eastern Province.

*Allied Species*
The **HOUSE MARTIN** (*Delichon urbica*) is another bird that travels thousands of miles on migration and is thus a well-known and welcome arrival. It is blue-black above with a conspicuous white rump; the underparts are white apart from the short forked tail which is black. The trailing edge of the underwing is black and the coverts white.

The **PALE CRAG MARTIN** (*Hirundo obsoleta*) breeds in the centre in one or two rocky areas and also in mountainous and hilly country in other parts of the peninsula. A small grey-brown bird whose pale fawn underparts fade to whitish on chin and throat. The darker, cleft tail has a line of white spots on the underside which are clearly visible as it swoops low around the cliffs. The wing coverts are paler than the flight feathers.

The **CRAG MARTIN** (*Hirundo rupestris*) is darker than the Pale Crag and the coverts are darker than the flight feathers. The throat is streaked dark and the tail is not cleft. It is an uncommon passage migrant, more often seen in spring than autumn.

are deeply forked and breeding males have long tail-streamers. When flying low, when their tails may be fanned, white spots at the tips of the inner feathers are clearly visible. Before leaving an area they will congregate in large numbers, assembling on rooftops and telephone wires. They are by no means silent and have a variety of calls and a twittering song. There are probably more 'old wive's tales' pertaining to the Swallow than any other bird. It is said they only breed under the eaves of houses in which there are children; farmers are said to expect rain 'when the swallows are flying low' and so on.

*Status in Central Arabia:* Passage migrant in large numbers; winter visitor in small numbers with an occasional straggler present throughout the summer.

*Status in Arabian Peninsula:* Passage migrant. Peak numbers in April and October and isolated breeding in Hejaz, the northwest and Bahrain.

## The **RED-RUMPED SWALLOW**
(*Hirundo daurica*) does not travel the enormous distances that the common swallow does and is not therefore so universally known. It is easily

*Fan-tailed Raven*, Corvus rhipidurus

The birds in this chapter belong to three families. They have little in common except that they are generally seen in flocks and are all perching birds.

Right: *Brown-necked Ravens.*

Below: *Brown-necked Raven in flight; note the tail shape.*

## BROWN-NECKED RAVEN
*Corvus ruficollis*
$19\frac{1}{2}$ inches (50cm)

*Identification:* The Brown-Necked Raven is an almost totally black bird that sometimes shows a tinge of brown on the neck and mantle, although this is not often very noticeable. They are wary and not easily approached though they can frequently be seen in groups of 10 to 15 in open desert or rocky country enjoying the remains of a dead camel or goat. In February and March groups of ravens can be seen 'dancing'

on the ground; they will take it in turns to jump into the air with outstretched wings, land immediately and watch the next one do the same thing. During the summer months they are generally seen with their bills wide open as if gulping in air. In the spring their large untidy nests are conspicuous in the middle of isolated thorn trees. Their voice is a raucous 'caw, caw, caw'.

*Habitat:* Open desert, generally near cliffs round which they can be seen gliding.

*Status in Central Arabia:* Very common, resident breeding. Observed in all months of the year.

*Status in Arabian Peninsula:* Probably breeding in most rocky interior areas but not commonly seen near the coast.

## FAN-TAILED RAVEN
*Corvus rhipidurus*
18½ inches (47cm)

*Identification:* This basically all-black bird can also show a tinge of brown. It is, however, readily distinguishable from the Brown-Necked by its very much shorter tail; when on the ground the tips of the wing protrude some way beyond the tail and when in flight the short, fanned tail and the very broad wings give it a distinct bat-like outline. The bill is heavier and, at close quarters, short bristles at the base are visible. Its voice is a shriller 'pruk, pruk'.

*Habitat:* By tall cliffs and escarpments, on which they nest.

*Status in Central Arabia:* Uncommon resident breeder.

*Status in Arabian Peninsula:* Resident breeding in Asir and in the mountainous areas of Hejaz.

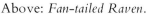

Above: *Fan-tailed Raven.*

Top right: *Fan-tailed Raven in flight; compare the tail shape with that of the Brown-necked Raven opposite.*

Above right: *Indian House Crow.*

## INDIAN HOUSE CROW
*Corvus splendens*
16 inches (40cm)

*Identification:* This rather sleek bird has a black mantle, black wings and tail, a black face and a black throat. It is a soft grey elsewhere.

*Habitat:* Towns, villages and by cultivation.

*Status in Arabian Peninsula:* Common resident breeder in Oman and UAE mountain areas. Occasional visitor to Hejaz, Bahrain and Kuwait.

*Allied Species*
The European **RAVEN** (*Corvus corax*) is present in small numbers in Asir. Much larger than the above ravens, it has an exceptionally heavy bill and a totally black plumage (25 inches/64cm).

The **MAGPIE** (*Pica pica*) is also found in Asir. This strikingly-marked black and white bird, with its very long irridescent greenish tail, is well-known in Europe, North America and the Orient.

## STARLING
*Sturnus vulgaris*
8½ inches (21.5cm)

*Identification:* In shade or under grey skies this bird looks dull and blackish. During the summer and when the sun is shining a sheen of purple and green transforms the bird into something nearly beautiful. They are heavily spotted on underparts and mantle, the spots being particularly noticeable in winter. The wings have bronze lights in them and, in flight against the sun,

*Status in Central Arabia:* Uncommon passage migrant and rare winter visitor.

*Status in Arabian Peninsula:* Common winter visitor in Eastern Province. Flocks of a hundred or so roost in tall trees in Dhahran. They are also present during the winter in the northwest and in Oman.

Below: *Starling in winter plumage. Although it occurs in vast flocks to the north, it is only a visitor to Arabia.*

*Allied Species*
The **ROSE-COLOURED STARLING** (*Sturnus roseus*) is a passage migrant in the southeastern parts of the peninsula. Its pink mantle and belly are sandwiched between the pure black of the rest of the body.

The beautiful **VIOLET-BACKED STARLING** (*Cinnyricinclus leucogaster*) is present in the mountainous parts of Hejaz and Asir. The upperparts of the male are irridescent violet-blue with a purplish

they appear almost transparent. The bill is brownish-yellow and the legs brownish-grey. In flight the shape of the bird is distinctive; the wings are short and wide at the base, narrowing quickly to very pointed tips. They are extremely gregarious and noisy – flocks let the neighbourhood know when they return to their trees to roost at sundown and again when they leave in the morning.

*Habitat:* Towns, villages, cultivated areas.

tinge in some lights; the throat and upper breast are the same and the rest of the underparts are pure white. Females and juveniles are brown above and white below with brown streaks on throat and breast.

## TRISTRAM'S GRACKLE
*Onycognathus tristramii*
10 inches (25cm)

*Identification:* The males have a shiny black plumage, while the females are duller with paler grey throats faintly streaked darker. Both sexes have a chestnut patch on the wing which is just visible on the edge of the folded wing when the bird is at rest and which is very conspicuous when in flight. The eye is dark red, the bill and the legs blackish. The call is a haunting '*Wheee*-too' with an occasional 'Wheet-a-weet'.

*Habitat:* Rocky cliffs and ravines among mountains. They have been occasionally observed on rooftops, road lamps and telegraph posts in Abha where they appear to have completely changed their usual habitat.

*Status in Arabian Peninsula:* Resident but very localised in mountainous areas of Hejaz and Asir.

## GOLDEN ORIOLE
*Oriolus oriolus*
9½ inches (24cm)

*Identification:* The male is quite unmistakable, being brilliant yellow with black wings and a yellow and black tail. The female is greeny-yellow with darker olive-green wings and paler streaked underparts. Both sexes have stout red bills and a black spot in front of the black eye, making the eye look very large and prominent. The call is a loud, melodious whistle. (It is interesting that there appears to be a race of orioles, similar in size to the Golden, present during migration that is different to that just described. They are referred to as 'Gypsy Orioles' by local Arabs who find them easy prey to their guns. Two of these birds have been observed by the author. The general appearance is grey and yellow. Head and neck are pale brownish-yellow; wings are pale soft grey; the belly and underwings are a bright, unstreaked yellow. The fairly stout bill is black and there is a prominent black eye.)

*Habitat:* Palm groves edged with tamarisk and beside water-filled wadis and lagoons. ('Gypsy' will frequent more open places and has been observed sunning itself on a rocky cliff.)

*Status in Central Arabia:* Passage migrant in small numbers – usually present when the dates are ripe in the groves.

*Status in Arabian Peninsula:* Uncommon passage migrant in several parts of the peninsula.

Left: *A pair of Tristram's Grackles.*

*Shrike's 'larder' – a Swallowtail Butterfly.*

These small-medium to medium sized birds have a beetle-browed appearance. They have longish, graduated tails and very strong-looking hooked bills. They are solitary and very aggressive. They are generally seen perched on the topmost branch of a small tree or bush, from which they swoop on to large insects or small vertebrates which they will impale on long thorns or on prongs of barbed wire using these as their 'larder' – hence their nickname of 'butcher birds'. Sexes are alike except for the Red-Backed and Isabelline.

faint bars on the breast; their colouring is the same as the adults except for the eyestripe which is grey not black and does not reach the bill. Their flight is undulating and the white on the black wing is very noticeable. This shrike is particularly strong and has been seen to attack and kill a nine-inch lizard by swooping onto it and digging into its throat. The alarm cry is loud and harsh; the song is soft, surprisingly musical and varied.

*Habitat:* Open sandy country where there is acacia.

**GREAT GREY SHRIKE**
*Lanius excubitor*
$9\frac{1}{2}$ inches (24cm)

*Identification:* The Great Grey Shrike is a striking black, white and silver-grey bird: silver-grey above, white below, black wings with white bars and a long black tail with white outer feathers and underside. There is a broad black eyestripe which runs *into* the black bill and a faint white stripe above the black. Juveniles have very

*Status in Central Arabia:* Resident breeding. Observed throughout the year, though in fewer numbers from March to September.

*Status in Arabian Peninsula:* Resident breeding in Hejaz, the northwest and UAE. Winter visitor and passage migrant in Eastern Province and the Gulf Coast.

Top: *Immature Great Grey Shrike.*

Above: *Great Grey Shrike.*

Left: *Lesser Grey Shrike.*

*Habitat:* Similar to Great Grey but perhaps one sees more of them out in desert country.

*Status in Central Arabia:* Winter visitor.

*Status in Arabian Peninsula:* Winter visitor and passage migrant in Hejaz, the northwest and Eastern Province.

## WOODCHAT SHRIKE
*Lanius senator*
$6\frac{3}{4}$ inches (17cm)

*Identification:* This beautiful shrike has a pale creamy front, bright chestnut head and nape, black wings with white bars and shoulder-patches. The very broad black eyestripe extends across the forehead *over* the bill and the tail, unlike the other shrikes, is partially black on the underside. In flight a white rump as well as prominent wing bars and shoulder patches make it easy to identify. It will perch on telegraph wires more often than other shrikes.

*Habitat:* Generally prefers the presence of trees and is therefore more often to be seen near cultivation, beside water-filled wadis and will occasionally visit town gardens.

*Status in Central Arabia:* Passage migrant.

*Status in Arabian Peninsula:* Passage migrant in Hejaz, the northwest, Eastern Province and the Gulf Coast.

## LESSER GREY SHRIKE
*Lanius minor*
8 inches (20cm)

*Identification:* The Lesser Grey Shrike is similar to the Great Grey but is a little smaller and generally distinguishable from it by a pinkish tinge on the breast and by the broader black eyestripe which continues *over* the bill; there is no white stripe above the black. The wings are shorter and the tail relatively longer. During the autumn the two Greys are extremely difficult to tell apart and at this time the simplest way to determine which is which is to note their posture when perched. The Lesser Grey is noticeably more erect on a branch than is the Great. The alarm cry and song are very similar though the former is even more raucous and the latter more variable.

Right: *Woodchat Shrike showing a chestnut crown and nape.*

## MASKED SHRIKE
*Lanius nubicus*
6¾ inches (17cm)

*Identification:* The upperparts of this shrike are almost completely black apart from white shoulder-patches which form a distinct 'V' on the back, and white outer edges to the black tail. It is the only shrike in the area with a white forehead. A broad black eyestripe separates the white forehead from the white chin and throat. The underparts are white with apricot at the sides of the breast and belly. It generally perches on lower branches than the Greys.

*Habitat:* Palm groves, water-filled wadis, tamarisks bordering cultivation and in gardens.

*Status in Central Arabia:* Passage migrant.

*Status in Arabian Peninsula:* Passage migrant in Hejaz, the northwest, Eastern Province and the Gulf Coast.

## RED-BACKED SHRIKE
*Lanius colurio*
6¾ inches (17cm)

*Identification:* The male has a grey crown and nape, browny-chestnut wings and mantle, a black upperside to the tail with white at each side of the base and a grey rump. The underparts are whitish, tinged with pink. A broad black eyestripe runs *into* the black bill. The female is brown with a suspicion of chestnut on the upperparts. Her breast and throat are well covered with crescent bars. Juveniles are greyish-brown with crescent markings on crown and mantle as well as breast. Due to the white at each side of its base, the tail resembles a small black club when the bird is in flight. They are extremely solitary birds – even when congregating in parties prior to migration it is rare to see two closer than 50 feet apart. A hen took up temporary residence in a thorn tree in the author's garden for two weeks one May and although her mate paid occasional visits to a nearby telegraph

wire to see how she was faring, he spent most of his time in a nearby empty lot.

*Habitat:* Roadsides, cultivated areas, beside permanent water and in gardens.

*Status in Central Arabia:* Passage migrant and winter visitor. Observed from August to May.

*Status in Arabian Peninsula:* Passage migrant in Hejaz, the northwest, Eastern Province and the Gulf Coast.

Top: *Masked Shrike.*          Above: *Male Red-backed Shrike.*

Left: *The female Red-backed Shrike is a much plainer bird than the male.*

Below: *Isabelline Shrike.*

## ISABELLINE SHRIKE
*Lanius isabellinus*
$6\frac{3}{4}$ inches (17cm)

*Identification:* The male is pale grey-brown above and pinkish-cream below. The wings are darker with whitish streaks and the tail is strikingly chestnut. He has a narrow black stripe through the eye with a suspicion of white above it. The female has almost no eyestripe and is very faintly barred on the breast. It generally perches on the ends of branches in the centre of a tree or bush.

*Habitat:* Similar to Red-Backed, which may be occupying one tree while Isabelline is in another twenty feet away.

*Status in Central Arabia:* As Red-Backed.

*Status in Arabian Peninsula:* Winter visitor and passage migrant in Hejaz and the northwest.

## 'RUFOUS' SHRIKE
*Lanius isabellinus phoenicuroides*
$6\frac{3}{4}$ inches (17cm)

This bird is the eastern race of the Isabelline and is the most beautiful shrike of the area. The mantle and wings are brown, the head and tail bright chestnut and the underparts are creamy-white. There is a narrow black stripe through the eye. The female is identical but is faintly barred on throat and breast. Her eyestripe contracts to a black spot behind the eye.

*Habitat:* Palm groves, cultivated areas and beside permanent water.

*Status in Central Arabia:* Passage migrant. Observed February to May and August to October.

*Status in Arabian Peninsula:* Passage migrant in Hejaz and the northwest. Winter visitor to Eastern Province, Bahrain, Oman and UAE.

Top: *Male 'Rufous' Shrike.*

Right: *Female 'Rufous' Shrike.*

# GREY HYPOCOLIUS
*Hypocolius ampelinus*
9 inches (23cm)

*Identification:* The male is a soft dove-grey from the back of the head to the tip of the long, narrow tail, the final half inch of which is black. The edge of the folded wing is black with white at the extreme tip, though this is not very noticeable. The underparts are pale pinkish-grey with a tinge of yellow at the sides of the breast and there is a broad black cheek patch narrowing into the thick, unhooked

*Habitat:* Semi-desert and dry wadis with acacia and in palm groves.

*Status in Central Arabia:* Winter visitor – localized.

*Status in Arabian Peninsula:* Breeds in Hejaz. Winter visitor in small numbers to Eastern Province.

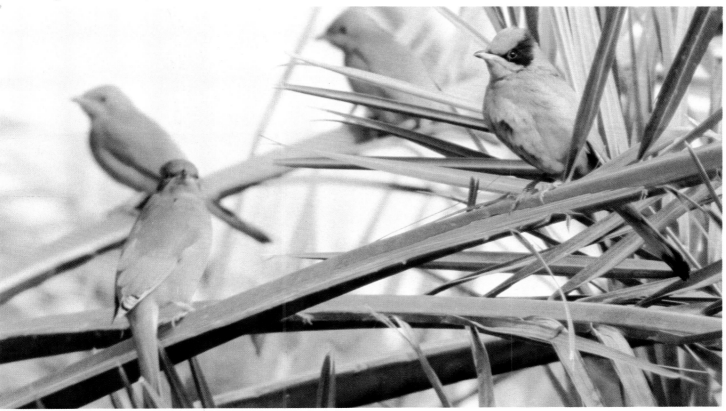

black bill. The colouring of the female is almost the same as the male but she is without black on the face or wing – she retains the very distinctive black on the tip of her tail. In flight the long tail fans out slightly and shows the distinct black tip and the white on the edge of the flight feathers is noticeable in good light. They are very active, gregarious and noisy. They emit a fairly continuous scolding chirp with occasional long drawn out whistles of 'pheeew', repeated two or three times.

Above: *Grey Hypocolius. The male is on the right, the female on the left foreground.*

*A rare white-throated form of the Pied Wheatear, Oenanthe pleschanka*

These small, neat birds are members of the large sub-family of *Turdidae* (Thrushes). With the exception of two (Red-Rumped and Red-Tailed) they all have very prominent white rumps. The tail pattern, which is generally only visible when the bird is in flight, is an important identification feature, as is the gap, if any, between the black of the throat and that of the wing. Females are, with a few exceptions, almost impossible to separate, most of them being brownish in colour with no identifying feature apart from the tail, which is the same as their mate. Juveniles are streaked paler. They are generally seen on the ground, on low rocks or on top of ridges in the sand. They seldom fly higher than a few feet from the ground.

Polymorphism (multiform, varying in individuals) is prevalent in one or two species which can make identification tricky but which makes wheatears among the most interesting birds in the area.

### EUROPEAN WHEATEAR
*Oenanthe oenanthe*
6 inches (15cm)

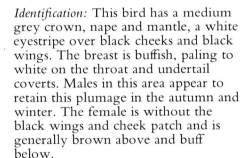

*Identification:* This bird has a medium grey crown, nape and mantle, a white eyestripe over black cheeks and black wings. The breast is buffish, paling to white on the throat and undertail coverts. Males in this area appear to retain this plumage in the autumn and winter. The female is without the black wings and cheek patch and is generally brown above and buff below.

*Habitat:* Sand or stony desert.

*Status in Central Arabia:* Winter visitor and passage migrant. Observed in small numbers in almost all months of the year with peak numbers in February/March and October.

*Status in Arabian Peninsula:* Winter visitor and passage migrant to most low-lying areas.

Top left: *European Wheatear.*

Top right: *Male Desert Wheatear.*

Above: *Female Desert Wheatear.*

## ISABELLINE WHEATEAR
*Oenanthe isabellina*
6½ inches (16.5cm)

*Identification:* The Isabelline Wheatear is sandy-grey above with darker streaking on the wings. The underparts are pale cream, darkening to buff on the breast. There is a distinct cream eyestripe. It is best distinguished from the females of the other species by its habit of running fast along the ground with head lowered and then stopping suddenly to stand tall and upright, wagging its tail furiously.

*Habitat:* Beside palm groves and cultivation.

*Status in Central Arabia:* Winter visitor.

*Status in Arabian Peninsula:* Winter visitor to most of peninsula and reported breeding in the west.

## DESERT WHEATEAR
*Oenanthe deserti*
6 inches (15cm)

*Identification:* The Desert Wheatear is a sandy-coloured bird with black cheeks and throat, black wings faintly streaked paler and a tail which is black to the base. The throat and wings are almost joined by a series of black spots on a white background. In flight the white on the inner edge of the wing coverts is fairly conspicuous and is diagnostic. The female is very similar to the female European and only the tail pattern separates them.

*Habitat:* Open sand or stony desert with little or no cover.

*Status in Central Arabia:* Winter visitor, present from September to early April.

*Status in Arabian Peninsula:* Winter visitor to Hejaz, the northwest, Eastern Province and Oman.

Top right: *Isabelline Wheatear.*

## BLACK-EARED WHEATEAR
*Oenanthe hispanica*
5¾ inches (14.5cm)

*Identification:* This bird is polymorphic with four forms. There is a brown form, a white form, a white-throated form and a black-throated form. Of the first two the paler form is the most common in this area. White throats and black throats are about even. On the black-throated form there is a clear gap between throat and wing, which separates it from the Desert Wheatear and from the Mourning and Pied.

*Habitat:* All kinds of desert and beside areas of desultory cultivation.

*Status in Central Arabia:* Passage migrant with a small number present during all winter months.

*Status in Arabian Peninsula:* Winter visitor in Hejaz, the northwest and UAE.

Centre: *Black-eared Wheatear.*
Left: *Black throated form of the Black-eared Wheatear.*

Below: *Male Pied Wheatear.*

Bottom: *Mourning Wheatear.*

Below: *Female Pied Wheatear.*
Opposite: *Rare white throated form of the Pied Wheatear.*

## MOURNING WHEATEAR

*Oenanthe lugens*
$5\frac{1}{4}$ inches (13.5cm)

*Identification:* This small black and white wheatear is distinguishable from all the others by its pinkish under-tail coverts. It has black cheeks and throat narrowly joined to the black wings and the mantle is black. The shade and the extent of the crown can vary enormously. On some birds it is very white and on others a pale grey. On some it is just a small cap and on others it is very deep indeed. The female is brownish grey above with a darker grey throat and dark grey wings streaked paler.

*Habitat:* Sand or stony desert with low shrubs.

*Status in Central Arabia:* Winter visitor.

*Status in Arabian Peninsula:* Winter visitor to Eastern Province and the northwest. Reported breeding in Hejaz.

## PIED WHEATEAR
*Oenanthe pleschanka*
5¾ inches (14.5cm)

*Identification:* This black and white wheatear can be confused with the pale form of the black-throated Black-Eared and also with the Mourning. It can be distinguished from the former by the strongly joined throat and wing, from the latter by the lack of pink on undertail coverts and from both by the yellow-apricot tinge on breast and flanks and the different tail pattern. While the great majority of these birds have a black throat, there is a very uncommon form with a white one. Again, while the majority have tails as illustrated here, some have much more black on them which can be confusing. Yet another complicating factor is that although the whole top of the head is white, in autumn and winter the feathers have blackish-brown fringes which often conceal the white and turn it into a rather scruffy grey. The female is brown above with darkish grey wings, streaked brown, and pale buff below darkening on the flanks.

*Habitat:* Beside wadis or cliffs with low bushes.

*Status in Central Arabia:* Winter visitor. Observed from September to April.

*Status in Arabian Peninsula:* Winter visitor to Hejaz, Eastern Province, the northwest and UAE.

## FINSCH'S WHEATEAR
*Oenanthe finschii*
5¼ inches (13.5cm)

*Identification:* This wheatear has a very pale grey crown which continues halfway down the back; at this point the mantle becomes white and joins the white rump. The black of cheeks and throat is broadly joined to the black wings. There is a faint white spot on the forewing which is apparent, when the bird is not too far away, both in flight and on the

ground. Its voice is an unusual grating rattle – 'Ch-rrrr-pt'.

*Habitat:* Stony desert and by escarpments.

*Status in Central Arabia:* Uncommon winter visitor.

*Status in Arabian Peninsula:* Uncertain. Reported occasionally in the northwest and Eastern Province.

Left: *Finsch's Wheatear.*

Below: *Male White-crowned Black Wheatear.*

## WHITE-CROWNED BLACK WHEATEAR
*Oenanthe leucopyga*
7 inches (17.5cm)

*Identification:* Apart from a shallow white crown, white rump and undertail coverts the male is totally black. The female and juvenile are almost identical but are without the white crown, though sometimes there is a faint lightening of the crown. As a result they can erroneously be identified as Black Wheatears which have tail markings as Hume's, Mourning and Finsch's and which are *not* present in the area. The very variable and musical song is uttered from a prominent rock and is extremely far-carrying.

*Habitat:* Wild open country beside rocky wadis and cliffs.

*Status in Central Arabia:* Resident breeding. Observed at all times of the year.

*Status in Arabian Peninsula:* Resident breeding in most parts of the area.

## RED-TAILED WHEATEAR
*Oenanthe xanthoprymna*
6½ inches (16.5cm)

*Identification:* This wheatear is a matt earthy-brown on its crown, nape, mantle and wings. The underparts are buffish-grey deepening to a reddish shade on its undertail coverts and base of tail. In flight the rump and base of its uppertail are markedly rufous.

*Habitat:* Rocky wadis and coastal cliffs.

*Status in Central Arabia:* Uncommon passage migrant.

*Status in Arabian Peninsula:* Winter visitor and passage migrant to eastern parts of the peninsula.

Left: *Female White-crowned Black Wheatear.*

Below: *Red-breasted Wheatear.*

## RED-BREASTED WHEATEAR
*Oenanthe bottae*
6 inches (15cm)

*Identification:* This generally dun-coloured wheatear has a pinkish-chestnut breast and dark edges to the folded wing. There is a prominent black line across the forehead which is variable in width. The tail is almost completely black having white only at the extreme base.

*Habitat:* Very general but only at higher altitudes.

*Status in Arabian Peninsula:* Common resident in several parts of Asir and around Taif in Hejaz. Localised.

*Allied Species*
**HUME'S WHEATEAR** (*Oenanthe alboniger*) was the first black and white wheatear to be seen by the author in Arabia but it is very uncommon in the centre although it breeds in Oman and the UAE mountains. It is distinguished by its totally black head and upperparts and is reminiscent of a tiny penguin. Its tail markings are the same as the Mourning.

The **HOODED WHEATEAR** (*Oenanthe monacha*) is an uncommon breeding bird in Nejd and Hejaz. It is similar to the White-Crowned Black but the belly is white as well as the undertail coverts. Its tail markings are the same as the White-Crowned. The female is brown with a slightly rufous tail.

The **RED-RUMPED WHEATEAR** (*Oenanthe moesta*) is an uncommon passage migrant to the centre, Eastern Province and UAE. It has a grey crown and nape, black throat and mantle and the black wings (firmly joined to the throat) are markedly streaked with grey and white. The rump, base of tail and the undertail coverts are rufous.

Left: *Red-tailed Wheatear.*

*Female Redstart,* Phoenicurus phoenicurus

The Thrush family is a large group of small to medium-sized insect-eating birds. Females are often duller than the males and the juveniles are spotted.

## SONG THRUSH
*Turdus philomelos*
9 inches (23cm)

*Identification:* This very familiar European bird is dark brown above, has an unmarked cream throat and heavily spotted underparts. The breast is tinged pale chestnut-brown and the belly is very pale cream. In flight the underwing coverts show pale chestnut. There is a pale stripe through the large black eye and the legs are brownish.

*Habitat:* Variable – palm groves, waste ground.

*Status in Central Arabia:* Uncommon winter visitor.

*Status in Arabian Peninsula:* Passage migrant and winter visitor in small numbers to most parts of the peninsula.

Top left: *Song Thrush.*

Above: *Black-Throated Thrush in winter.*

Above right: *Female Blue Rock Thrush.*
Top right: *Male Blue Rock Thrush.*

## BLACK-THROATED THRUSH
*Turdus ruficollis atrogularis*
9 inches (23cm)

*Identification:* The upperparts of this bird are blackish-brown; the underparts are off-white on the belly and pure white on undertail coverts which are very conspicuous as the bird cocks its tail. In summer the male has a pure black chin and throat; in winter this is partly obscured by pale fringes. The female has a whitish throat with a

band of speckled brown across the upper breast.

*Habitat:* Cultivated areas and beside water-filled wadis.

*Status in Central Arabia:* Uncertain. Occasional birds observed in September and November.

*Status in Arabian Peninsula:* Uncommon winter visitor in eastern parts of peninsula.

The **ROCK THRUSH** (*Monticola saxatilis*) is a passage migrant, seen more often in spring than autumn, to most parts of the peninsula. The head and upperparts of the male are a brighter blue-grey than the Blue Rock Thrush and the lower part of the back is almost white. The underparts from below the throat are reddish-chestnut and the tail deep chestnut. The female is paler brown than her Blue counterpart and has a rufous tail.

The **YEMEN THRUSH** (*Turdus menachensis*) is probably resident in Asir. It is a shy bird and keeps to well-wooded wadis. It is olive-brown above and pale olive-grey below with dark brown streaks on throat and breast; there is a rusty tinge to the flanks and the underwing has a touch of rufous. The eyes are orange and the bill yellow.

## BLUE ROCK THRUSH
*Monticola solitarius*
8 inches (20cm)

*Identification:* The male is bluish-grey all over, darker on the wings and tail. The female is much browner and finely barred with buff from chin to undertail coverts. Immature males are lightly barred on the breast. They are very solitary birds.

*Habitat:* Anywhere where there are rocks, cliffs or ruins.

*Status in Central Arabia:* Winter visitor.

*Status in Arabian Peninsula:* Winter visitor and passage migrant to most parts of the peninsula.

Above: *Male Blackstart.*    Top right: *Female Blackstart.*

## BLACKSTART
*Cercomela melanura*
6 inches (15cm)

*Identification:* The Blackstart is a slim, chic little bird. The male is soft grey above, paler below and whitening at undertail coverts; the wings are a darker grey and the rump and tail (which is fanned and cocked occasionally when perched) are black. The female is a brownish-grey and also has a black tail.

*Habitat:* Stony desert with acacia or tamarisk, in dry wadis and beside escarpments.

*Status in Central Arabia:* Resident breeding. Observed in large numbers from February to May and in smaller numbers at other times of the year.

*Status in Arabian Peninsula:* This bird is not known in eastern parts of the peninsula but is probably resident in Hejaz and the northwest.

Below: *Female Redstart.*

Right: *Male Redstart.*

Above: *Black Redstart.*

## REDSTART
*Phoenicurus phoenicurus samamisicus*
$5\frac{1}{2}$ inches (14cm)

*Identification:* The breeding male is a smooth dark grey above with darker wings on which there is a white patch. The face and throat are black and the forehead white. The breast is rufous paling to creamish-apricot at undertail coverts and the tail is bright chestnut with darker feathers in the centre. The non-breeding male and the female have a deep olive-brown mantle and wings, the latter being streaked dark and light at the edge, and pale cream underparts. The tail is dark brown in the centre with brilliant chestnut on the outer feathers and on the upper and lower tail coverts. When perched there is a constant shivering play of the tail and at the same time they utter a frequent 'tck-tck-tck'.

*Habitat:* Palm groves and tamarisks.

*Status in Central Arabia:* Probably a winter visitor though one or two have been observed in most months of the year.

*Status in Arabian Peninsula:* Winter visitor and passage migrant.

## BLACK REDSTART
*Phoenicurus ochrurus*
$5\frac{1}{2}$ inches (14cm)

*Identification:* An almost black bird (grey-brown in the female), the Black Redstart has a brilliant chestnut rump and tail. The Middle East race, *P. o. phoenicuroides* is very much more frequently seen however. The male is very dark grey on his crown and mantle with even darker wings. The face, throat and breast are pure black and the belly, tail and upper and lower tail coverts are bright chestnut. There is a faint lightening on the forehead. The female is brownish grey on head, mantle, throat and breast. There is a constant shivering of the tail.

*Habitat:* Palm groves, tamarisks bordering cultivation.

*Status in Central Arabia:* The nominate race occurs much less frequently than the Middle East variety. The former is probably a passage migrant and the latter a winter visitor.

*Status in Arabian Peninsula:* Winter visitor and passage migrant to Asir, Hejaz, Eastern Province, UAE and Oman.

## BLACK BUSH ROBIN/CHAT
*Cercotrichas podobe*
10 inches (25cm)

*Identification:* This bird is almost completely black with a very long graduated tail which it sometimes cocks up well above the head, sometimes fans out and sometimes trails along the ground. When the tail is cocked a long double line of rather smudgy white marks are visible on the underside. Eyes, short down-curved bill and legs are black. In flight the tail is often well fanned and there is a white spot at the tip of all but the

## RUFOUS BUSH CHAT
*Cercotrichas galactotes syriacus*
6½ inches (16cm)

*Identification:* This plain greyish-brown bird has a really beautiful tail which it cocks up, fans and flicks. This not-very-long graduated tail is dark chestnut-brown and the tips of all but the central feathers are each decorated with a white and a black spot. The eye is black with a dark streak running through and there is a cream-coloured bar above. Underparts are creamy white and the undertail coverts are white and very prominent when the tail is cocked. There are very faint and indistinct creamy patches on the undertail.

*Habitat:* Palm groves and in shrubs bordering cultivation or water-filled wadis.

*Status in Central Arabia:* Summer visitor, breeding.

*Status in Arabian Peninsula:* Breeds in Eastern Province and is a passage migrant in Oman.

## WHITE-THROATED ROBIN
*Irania gutturalis*
7 inches (18cm)

*Identification:* A very shy and retiring bird, the White-Throated Robin is generally seen in the middle of a thick shrub or low tree. The male is dark grey above with a black tail which is often cocked; the cheeks are black and there is a white eyestripe. Underparts are rufous shading to cream at undertail coverts. The narrow patch of white on the throat is only noticeable when the bird is seen from the front. The female is grey on her head and upperparts; she has a yellowish brown breast and a cream belly; her tail is black and the undertail coverts show very white when the tail is cocked. The song is penetrating and bell-like and there is a low rattling sound made from under a favourite bush.

*Habitat:* Variable. Although only observed infrequently, on each occasion it has been in a different type of habitat. Stony areas with cover, palm groves and small gardens.

*Status in Central Arabia:* Passage migrant or winter visitor in small numbers.

*Status in Arabian Peninsula:* Passage migrant in Hejaz and Eastern Province.

Top: *Rufous Bushchat.*

Above: *Black Bush Robin.*
Below: *White-throated Robin.*

central tail feathers. Also noticeable in flight is a chestnut patch on the underwing. The song is a double-note musical whistle.

*Habitat:* Palm groves.

*Status in Central Arabia:* Resident breeding in one or two selected palm groves. Deep, well-built nests have been found by the author in the centre of pomegranate trees.

*Status in Arabian Peninsula:* Breeds in Hejaz.

## BLUETHROAT
*Luscinia svecica magna*
5½ inches (14cm)

*Identification:* These little birds are earth-brown on the head, mantle and wings, off-white on the belly and have a brown tail which is rufous at the base. The breeding male has a sky-blue throat and upper breast, a fairly broad band of red on the lower breast and a narrow black line dividing the blue from the red. Non-breeding males and females are without the red and the blue is less extensive and duller. They seem very unafraid and can be approached with comparative ease.

*Habitat:* Reed beds, palm groves and well-watered areas of cultivation.

*Status in Central Arabia:* Winter visitor in small numbers.

*Status in Arabian Peninsula:* Winter visitor and passage migrant to Asir, Hejaz and the Gulf Coast.

## THRUSH NIGHTINGALE
*Luscinia luscinia*
6½ inches (16.5cm)

*Identification:* The head, mantle and wings are a dark earthy-brown; the throat is off-white and the underparts pale brownish-grey with faint darker spots on the breast and a rufous tinge at the sides of the belly and on the flanks. The tail is dark chestnut-brown and there is a faint white circle round the eye. It can often be seen perched on a prominent post or branch from where it will dive swiftly into the centre of a bush as the watcher approaches.

*Habitat:* Areas with plenty of cover, generally close to water.

*Status in Central Arabia:* Passage migrant in small numbers.

*Status in Arabian Peninsula:* Uncommon passage migrant in Asir, Hejaz and the Gulf Coast.

Above: *Bluethroat.*

Right: *Male Stonechat.*

Below: *Thrush Nightingale.*

The **NIGHTINGALE** (*Luscinia megarhynchos*) is an uncommon migrant reported in most parts of the peninsula. It is a paler brown than the Thrush Nightingale, is lightly streaked, rather than spotted, on the breast and has a redder tail.

## STONECHAT
*Saxicola torquata*
5 inches (13cm)

*Identification:* These small robin-like members of the thrush family perch very upright on tops of small bushes, pieces of long grass or on prominent rocks. The male has a black head, mantle, wings and tail, has deep apricot on the breast and a cream belly. There is a white half collar, a white wing bar and white rump. The race seen most frequently in Central Arabia is *S. t. varigata* which has very much more white on the wing and a deep white collar right round the neck.

*Habitat:* Almost anywhere but seldom close to human habitation.

*Status in Central Arabia:* Winter visitor. Observed in all months of the year except May and June.

*Status in Arabian Peninsula:* Winter visitor and passage migrant to most parts of the peninsula.

## WHINCHAT
*Saxicola rubetra*
5 inches (13cm)

*Identification:* This bird has similar colouring to the Stonechat but can easily be distinguished by the lack of black head and throat. The male has a prominent long white eyestripe and a black cheek; the brown crown and mantle are speckled with black and there is white at either side of the base of the black tail. The female is very like the female Stonechat but has no brown on the throat and she has a distinct cream eyestripe. Both sexes have a white wing bar.

*Habitat:* Open country but likes water nearby.

*Status in Central Arabia:* Passage migrant in small numbers.

*Status in Arabian Peninsula:* Uncommon passage migrant to Eastern Province.

Above: *Female Stonechat.*

Below left: *Male Stonechat (Nejd race).*
Below right: *Female Whinchat.*

113

*Tawny Pipit,* Anthus campestris

Members of this group of slim, long-tailed terrestrial birds seldom perch on trees or shrubs and are more commonly sighted on the ground.

Below: *Tawny Pipit.*

## TAWNY PIPIT
*Anthus campestris*
6½ inches (16cm)

*Identification:* The adult bird is the only pipit of the region that has no streaking on the breast. It is a sandy-brown colour, lightly streaked on the crown and on the wings; underparts are paler and the dark tail has cream outer feathers. The legs are variable in colour, ranging from pale flesh to quite a deep pink. There is a short pale stripe behind the eye with a darkish cheek triangle below. This bird shows its relationship to the wagtails by its habit of frequently bobbing its head and tail. Juveniles are darker and streaked on the breast.

*Habitat:* Open stony country.

*Status in Central Arabia:* Passage migrant and possibly winter visitor in small numbers.

*Status in Arabian Peninsula:* Winter visitor in small numbers to several inland areas.

## TREE PIPIT
*Anthus trivialis*
6 inches (15cm)

*Identification:* This pipit is very heavily streaked on its sand-coloured breast; the throat and belly are cream and the upperparts are brown, streaked black on the head and black and white on the wings. A cheek triangle is formed within a cream stripe through the eye and another one below. The legs are pink. It is the most aerial of the pipits.

*Habitat:* By palm groves and cultivation bordered by tamarisks.

*Status in Central Arabia:* Passage migrant and winter visitor in small numbers.

*Status in Arabian Peninsula:* Passage migrant to Hejaz, the northwest, Eastern Province and UAE.

Left: *Tree Pipit.*

Below: *Red-throated Pipit.*

**RED-THROATED PIPIT**
*Anthus cervinus*
5¾ inches (14.5cm)

*Identification:* In summer plumage this bird can be distinguished from all other pipits by its red throat and breast – the extent and shade of red varies considerably from one bird to the next and some are streaked and some are not. In winter the throat and belly are creamish, streaked black. In all seasons the crown, mantle and wings are markedly streaked. Legs and bill are pale brown and there is a lot of white on the outer tail feathers.

*Habitat:* Beside water-filled wadis and in well-irrigated palm groves.

*Status in Central Arabia:* Winter visitor. Observed in both plumages.

*Status in Arabian Peninsula:* Winter visitor in Hejaz, the northwest, Eastern Province and UAE.

*Allied Species*
The **MEADOW PIPIT** (*Anthus pratensis*) is a winter visitor to the northwest and Eastern Province and has been reported occasionally in central Arabia. It can be distinguished from the Tree Pipit by its duller colour and darker legs.

The **WATER** or **ROCK PIPIT** (*Anthus spinoletta*) is an uncommon passage migrant to the centre and a winter visitor to the northwest and the Gulf Coast. It can be distinguished by its much greyer plumage and blackish legs.

117

## WHITE WAGTAIL
*Motacilla alba*
7 inches (18cm)

*Identification:* This small black, grey and white bird has a long black tail edged with white. In all seasons the mantle and rump are a medium shade of soft grey, the face is white and the crown black. In winter there is a narrow black bib below the white throat; in summer the bib extends to cover chin and throat. The juvenile is grey without black on the crown and with just a small black bib. On the ground their gait is fast and jerky; when stationary they constantly bob their head and tail. During the daytime they seldom fly any distance but, when they do (generally at nightfall and sunrise, when large flocks may pass overhead) they have a long bounding flight, generally accompanied by song – '*ti*-zak, *ti*-zak'.

*Habitat:* Almost anywhere – gardens, roadside, beside cultivation and particularly near water.

*Status in Central Arabia:* Winter visitor and passage migrant.

*Status in Arabian Peninsula:* Winter visitor to all parts.

## GREY WAGTAIL
*Motacilla cinerea*
7 inches (18cm)

*Identification:* The Grey Wagtail is slighter than the white and with a proportionately longer tail. It can be distinguished from the Yellow Wagtail by its *grey* head and mantle. The male in summer plumage is a brilliant yellow below apart from a pure black throat. The female and winter-plumaged male are without the black throat and the yellow is not so intense. In February and March males have been observed with soft grey throats. The juvenile is grey above, white below with just a tinge of yellow at the sides of the breast and on the flanks and undertail coverts. On the ground the constant wagging of the head and very long tail is reminiscent of a children's see-saw. The flight is less bounding and less often accompanied by their (monosyllabic) flight-call.

*Habitat:* Always by water.

*Status in Central Arabia:* Passage migrant.

*Status in Arabian Peninsula:* Passage migrant in the northwest, Eastern Province and Oman.

Above: *Juvenile White Wagtail.*

Above: *White Wagtail.*

Above: *Grey Wagtail.*

## YELLOW WAGTAIL
*Motacilla flava*
6½ inches (16.5cm)

*Identification:* The Yellow Wagtail can be distinguished from the Grey by its olive-green mantle and by its very much shorter tail. Apart from these two unalterable features the breeding males vary enormously, mainly in head pattern which is different in each of the many races. In a large group one late March afternoon four different races were observed together. The most common is the Blue-Headed which has a strikingly blue head, olive-green mantle, dark grey wings streaked white, a black tail edged with white and brilliant yellow on throat, breast and belly. Second commonest is the Black-Headed which has been observed with and without a white eyestripe. Females and non-breeding males have greenish grey heads and mantles and their underparts can by anything from pure white through cream to pale yellow.

*Habitat:* Beside water or in meadows, near cultivation.

*Status in Arabian Peninsula:* Present throughout the year in most areas with peak numbers in March/April and September/October

Above left: *Blue-headed Yellow Wagtail.*

Below left: *Black-headed Yellow Wagtail.*

*Allied Species*
## The CITRINE WAGTAIL
(*Motacilla citreola*) has been recorded in the northwest, Eastern Province and Hejaz. It is unmistakable, having a brilliant yellow head as well as underparts.

Larks are small to medium song-birds with sober, generally brown colouring. For their size they are heavy-looking and their wings are broad. On the ground they run or walk but do not hop. Apart from the Finch-Lark the sexes are alike.

## HOOPOE LARK
*Alaemon alaudipes*
$7\frac{1}{2}$ inches (19cm)

*Identification:* One of the bigger larks and very distinctive, the Hoopoe Lark is smooth brown above, white below with rows of dark streaking on upper breast. The long dark bill is down-curved; the edge of the wing and the outer tail feathers are black. In flight the underwing is whitish with broad black tips and on the upperwing there is a very striking black and white wing pattern. As the bird flutters not far from the ground it is reminiscent of a very large butterfly. They have a beautiful and quite unmistakable song, starting with a musical whistle and ending with a series of bell-like notes which can be heard from a great distance. They run very fast along the ground and when they stop, have a very upright stance although on one occasion a bird was observed by the author actually lying down under a low shrub. In late April and early May, if one is lucky, one can witness the male's aerial display. He spirals vertically up into the air, drops down with spread wings and finally plummets to the ground almost exactly from where he took off; during the fall his bell-like notes can be heard loud and clear.

*Habitat:* Sand or stony desert with low shrubs.

*Status in Central Arabia:* Resident, breeding.

*Status in Arabian Peninsula:* Resident breeding.

Above: *Hoopoe Lark.*

## BLACK-CROWNED FINCH-LARK
*Eremopterix nigriceps*
$4\frac{1}{2}$ inches (11cm)

*Identification:* These very small birds are really more like finches than larks as they have the short thick bill characteristic of the former. However on the ground they walk or run and do not hop as a finch would do. The male is very distinctive, having a black head with a broad white cheek patch below the eye and a small white patch on the forehead. The nape, mantle and wings are lightly-streaked sandy-brown and his entire underparts are pure black as are the outer feathers of his otherwise brown tail. The underwing is also black and from below he appears a small, totally black bird. The female, if it were not for the fact that she is never far from her mate, would be very difficult to spot as she is pale sandy-coloured with black outer tail feathers.

*Habitat:* Sand or stony desert with sparse vegetation.

*Status in Central Arabia:* Summer visitor and possibly resident in small numbers.

*Status in Arabian Peninsula:* Resident, breeding in Hejaz and in Eastern Province.

Left: *Lesser Short-toed Lark.*

Below left: *Black-crowned Finch-Lark.*

## LESSER SHORT-TOED LARK
*Calandrella rufescens*
$5\frac{1}{2}$ inches (14cm)

*Identification:* The pale brown upperparts are completely covered in dark grey-brown streaks. Underparts are whitish apart from brown streaks on the breast. Legs and bill are brownish-yellow and there is a pale stripe through the eye. The brown tail has black outer feathers. It could well be mistaken for a pipit but it has a shorter bill and shorter legs.

*Habitat:* Scrub or stony desert with water nearby.

*Status in Central Arabia:* Has been known to breed but generally only after wet winters. Very small numbers have been observed in most months of the year.

*Status in Arabian Peninsula:* Breeds in Eastern Province. Winter visitor and passage migrant in lower parts of Asir and in Oman.

The **SHORT-TOED LARK**
(*Calandrella cinerea*) breeds in Hejaz and is a winter visitor and passage migrant to the centre and to eastern parts of the peninsula. It is very similar to the Lesser Short-Toed Lark but is not so grey and does not have any streaking on the breast. The top of the head is rufous.

## TEMMINCK'S HORNED LARK
(*Eremophila bilopha*) is a very uncommon resident breeder in Central Arabia and Kuwait. It is an unstreaked sandy-coloured bird with a white face decorated with three black bands. From the sides of the top (shortest) bar protrude short, narrow black 'horns'. The tail is brown in the centre with black outer feathers.

123

## CRESTED LARK
*Galerida cristata*
6¾ inches (17cm)

*Identification:* This brown bird is heavily streaked with black on its upperparts. The crest is very prominent when on the ground and it stands very upright and proud-looking on the tops of banks or low rocks. The underparts are creamy with brown streaks on the breast and the tail is black with brown outer feathers. The colour of the legs varies greatly – from a nondescript sandy colour to quite a deep pink. In flight an orange-buff patch is visible on the underwing and they seem larger and heavier than when on the ground.

*Habitat:* Very general but not often near trees or habitation.

*Status in Central Arabia:* Very common. Resident breeding.

*Status in Arabian Peninsula:* Resident breeding in all low-lying areas.

## DESERT LARK
*Ammomanes deserti*
5¾ inches (15cm)

*Identification:* This uniform sandy-brown lark has rufous on the edge of the folded wing, dark feathers at the tip of the wing and a fairly long warm brown tail which darkens slightly at the tip. The rather thick bill and the legs are yellowish-brown.

*Habitat:* Anywhere where cliffs rise from the desert. Generally found on slightly higher ground than Bar-Tailed.

*Status in Central Arabia:* Common resident breeding.

*Status in Arabian Peninsula:* Resident breeding in most areas where there are mountains or rocky cliffs.

Top: *Crested Lark.*          Above: *Desert Lark.*

## BAR-TAILED DESERT LARK
*Ammomanes cincturus*
$5\frac{1}{4}$ inches (13cm)

*Identification:* The Bar-Tailed Desert Lark is a plumper-looking bird than the Desert and has a thinner and more pointed little bill. It is otherwise very similar in colouring but is faintly streaked on the breast and on the top of the head, has a shorter tail (not noticeably barred at the tip) and the legs are generally a little darker. There is a suspicion of a white ring round the eye.

*Habitat:* Sandy desert, not found on cliffs.

*Status in Central Arabia:* Fairly common and probably breeding.

*Status in Arabian Peninsula:* Breeds in Eastern Province.

## DUNN'S LARK
*Ammomanes dunni*
6 inches (15cm)

*Identification:* Similar to the Desert and the Bar-Tailed Desert, the Dunn's Lark is slimmer and has a longer uniformly dark brown tail. The crown is streaked, the mantle is scaly-looking and there are faint streaks on the breast. The yellow bill is not as thick as the Desert's but thicker than Bar-tailed.

*Habitat:* Generally in more wooded or cultivated areas than the other two.

*Status in Central Arabia:* Fairly common and probably breeding.

*Status in Arabian Peninsula:* Breeds in Eastern Province.

Above: *Dunn's Lark.*       Top: *Bar-tailed Desert Lark.*

# 13 Finches and Other Finch-like Birds

*Sparrows at Layla*

All these small birds have short, thick seed-eating bills and, unlike the larks, will hop when on the ground. Many of the common European finches (Goldfinch, Greenfinch, Chaffinch, Brambling and Serin for example) are present in the peninsula, particularly in the northwest and more northern parts of the Gulf Coast area. Since, however, they are well covered in books of European birds and are not known in the main bulk of the peninsula they are not included in this volume.

## TRUMPETER FINCH
*Rhodopechys githaginea*
5 inches (13cm)

*Identification:* The breeding male has an unmistakable red bill and a pale reddish tinge to his brown body. The typically short stubby bill of non-breeding males and all females is yellow; the plumage is dull brown with a very slight suspicion of pink and markedly contrasting dark tips to the wings and a dark tail. Often seen in threes, one male and two females, they are always on the ground busily

Above: *Trumpeter Finch.*
Below: *Yemen Linnet.*

pecking for seed; when disturbed they will fly a short distance and immediately continue the hunt.

*Habitat:* Dry wadis, escarpments and open stony desert.

*Status in Central Arabia:* Resident breeding but they are far less common than they appeared to be a few years ago.

*Status in Arabian Peninsula:* Resident breeding in Hejaz, the northwest and Eastern Province.

The **SINAI ROSE-FINCH** (*Carpodacus synoicus*) is probably breeding in one or two very localised spots in the northwest. The male has a bright pink head, rump and underparts with white streaks on the face and throat. The mantle, wings and tail are brown and the bill yellowish. The female is brown faintly tinged with pink.

## YEMEN LINNET
*Carduelis yemenensis*
5 inches (13cm)

*Identification:* The male has a blue-grey head, reddish-brown upperparts, a black and grey tail with white outer-feathers and a grey rump. The underparts are creamish with pink below the grey throat, pinkish-brown on the sides of the breast and slightly apricot on the flanks. The female is browner but otherwise very similar. There are streaks of black, white and pink on the folded wing. In flight the birds resemble large butterflies, having very fast wing movement and there is a broad white patch on both sides of the wing which is very conspicuous as they fly overhead, generally uttering a thin tinkling 'ree-ee-ee' as they go.

*Habitat:* High altitudes – anywhere with trees or cultivation of any kind.

*Status in Arabian Peninsula:* Common resident in Asir.

## HOUSE SPARROW
*Passer domesticus*
5¾ inches (14.5cm)

*Identification:* There can be very few parts of the globe where this ubiquitous little bird is not part of the daily scene. They are the typical 'little brown birds' that are never far from human habitation. Their chirping and cheeping during daylight hours is almost non-stop. Around Riyadh they can frequently be seen somehow clinging on to the walls of houses apparently finding plenty to eat on these surfaces.

Below: *Male House Sparrow.*
Bottom: *Female House Sparrow.*

*Habitat:* Anywhere and everywhere.

*Status throughout the Arabian Peninsula:* Common resident breeding.

## RUPPELL'S WEAVER
*Ploceus galbula*
6 inches (14 cm)

*Identification:* The breeding male has a bright yellow crown, neck and underparts with dark reddish-brown on chin, cheeks and forehead; upperparts are yellowish-green with yellow bars on the wing. The non-breeding male and the female are similar to the female House Sparrow with a yellowish tinge on the breast, greenish on the head and mantle and olivaceous on the wings and tail.

*Habitat:* Wooded wadis and more open country where there are trees.

*Status in Arabian Peninsula:* Resident breeding in Asir and Hejaz.

Top: *Ruppell's Weaver nest.*
Above: *Ruppell's Weaver.*

## HOUSE BUNTING
*Emberiza striolata*
5½ inches (14cm)

*Identification:* 'House' Bunting is a strange name for this bird which, in this part of the world, is only to be found in remote areas far away from houses of any description. The male has a warm reddish brown plumage with a contrasting blue-grey head marked conspicuously with long white stripes and less conspicuous black ones. The female is a paler version of the male without the head pattern. The birds observed in Asir had blue-grey heads but were without the conspicuous stripes.

*Habitat:* Dry wadis and below escarpments; occasionally found perched on the wall of a well after having had a drink.

*Status in Central Arabia:* Resident breeding in fairly small numbers.

*Status in Arabian Peninsula:* Resident breeding in most parts of the peninsula.

Top: *Ortolan Bunting.*
Above: *House Bunting.*

Above: *Female Reed Bunting.*

## ORTOLAN
*Emberiza hortulana*
6½ inches (16.5cm)

*Identification:* This bunting has a greenish-grey head, nape and breast with a yellow moustacial stripe and throat; there is a white ring round the eye. The rest of the body is reddish-brown streaked darker on the wing and unstreaked, paler and pinker on the belly. The tail is dark. The female is paler with less green in the grey of the head. Both sexes have the distinctive red-orange bill and legs.

*Habitat:* Cultivated areas and beside permanent water.

*Status in Central Arabia:* Uncommon passage migrant.

*Status in Arabian Peninsula:* Passage migrant in Hejaz, the northwest, Eastern Province and UAE.

## REED BUNTING
*Emberiza schoeniclus*
6 inches (15cm)

*Identification:* Only non-breeding males are found in the peninsula. He is brown, streaked black above, off-white below with brown streaks on breast and flanks and has a grey head and throat with a white moustacial stripe. Females have brown heads with a black moustacial stripe, a white half-collar and white throat and short eye-stripe.

*Habitat:* Fresh water with reed beds and mossy banks.

*Status in Arabian Peninsula:* Uncommon winter visitor in Eastern Province and Bahrain.

# 14 Warblers and Other Small Birds

*Willow Warbler*, Phylloscopus trochilus

# Warblers (Sylviidae)

This large family of very active, insect-eating little birds has a slender bill and fairly sober plumage – grey, olive, brown or black above and cream, yellow or pale grey below. The birds are divided into several groups and the species within each group can be confusingly similar. Sexes are alike except for those in the Sylvia group. Juveniles are unspotted.

Above: *Reed Warbler.*

Right: *Great Reed Warbler.*

**REED WARBLERS** *Acrocephalus.* Reed Warblers are characterised by broad, very rounded tails, very thin, sharp bills and rather high foreheads.

## REED WARBLER
*Acrocephalus scirpaceus*
5 inches (12.5cm)

*Identification:* The Reed Warbler is a warm olive-brown above, has paler greyish underparts and a pale chestnut rump. There is a faint fawn stripe running through the black eye and the legs are dark grey. Voice is a thin 'eet-eet, eet-eet, eet'.

*Habitat:* Reeds or tamarisk beside permanent water. On one or two occasions single Reed Warblers have spent a few hours, completely still, on a branch of a thorn tree in the author's garden in the centre of Riyadh.

*Status in Central Arabia:* Passage migrant. With the growth of reed beds in the newly formed lakes and streams fed by sewage outflow it is probable they may visit the area in greater numbers.

*Status in Arabian Peninsula:* Passage migrant where there is suitable habitat.

## GREAT REED WARBLER
*Acrocephalus arundinaceus*
7½ inches (18cm)

*Identification:* It is hard to credit, when observing this very much bigger bird, that it is indeed a warbler. The shape of the head and, in particular, the broad, rounded tail as well as its reddish-olive plumage and prominent pale eyestripe are diagnostic features. The tips of the wings have short, curved dark bars. The gape is dark red. Voice is a loud croaking 'urrk-urrk-urrk'.

*Habitat:* Reeds or tamarisk by permanent water.

*Status in Central Arabia:* Passage migrant.

*Status in Arabian Peninsula:* Uncommon passage migrant in the northwest and Eastern Province.

## CLAMOROUS REED WARBLER

*Acrocephalus stentoreus*
7¼ inches (18cm)

*Identification:* The Clamorous Reed Warbler is very similar to the Reed Warbler but its colouring has more grey than chestnut to the brown and the bill is very much flatter and longer. It has a habit of moving from spot to spot among the mangrove stumps with distinct hops and is very noisy as it busily moves around.

*Habitat:* Mangroves or similar beds.

*Status in Central Arabia:* Uncommon passage migrant during the autumn.

*Status in Arabian Peninsula:* Passage migrant in Eastern Province and winter visitor (possibly resident) in Oman.

The **SEDGE WARBLER** (*Acrocephalus schoenobaenus* – 5 inches/12.5cm) is a passage migrant to most parts of the peninsula. The same size as the Reed it is streaked black on its head, mantle and wings and has a prominent white eyestripe. The rump is chestnut and unstreaked.

The **MOUSTACHED WARBLER** (*Acrocephalus melanopogon*) is reported to breed occasionally in Eastern Province and is a passage migrant there and in the northwest. It can be separated from the Sedge by a darker

Above: *Olivaceous Warbler.*

Below: *Clamorous Reed Warbler. Compare this with the other Acrocephalus species opposite.*

crown and cheek patch and by a chestnut tinge on the mantle and wings between the dark streaks.

**HIPPOLAIS WARBLERS** The Hippolais Warblers are characterised by the squared end to the tail, rather flat bills and highish foreheads. When alarmed they will raise the feathers on the crown.

## OLIVACEOUS WARBLER

*Hippolais pallida*
5¼ inches (13.5cm)

*Identification:* This bird is unstreaked olive-grey all over, slightly darker above than below. The black eye has a very faint pale stripe running through it and there are slightly paler streaks on the wing. Its legs and bill are much the same colour as the rest of the bird.

*Habitat:* Orchards and gardens.

*Status in Central Arabia:* Passage migrant in large numbers and uncommon summer visitor breeding.

*Status in Arabian Peninsula:* Breeds in Eastern Province and Bahrain. Passage migrant in most areas.

## ICTERINE WARBLER
*Hippolais icterina*
$5\frac{1}{4}$ inches (13.5cm)

*Identification:* A pretty little bird, the Icterine Warbler has olive-green upperparts, and is streaked dark and pale on the wing. The underparts are yellow and there is a yellow stripe through the eye. The legs are dark and the bill pinkish-grey.

*Habitat:* Tamarisks bordering cultivation and water-filled wadis.

Above: *Compare the shape of the head of this Icterine Warbler with that of the* Phylloscopus *species such as the Chiffchaff and Willow Warbler. Note the flatter forehead and longer bill.*

*Status in Central Arabia:* Uncommon passage migrant.

*Status in Arabian Peninsula:* Uncommon passage migrant in Eastern Province.

*Allied Species*
**UPCHER'S WARBLER** (*Hippolais languida*) is an uncommon passage migrant to central and Gulf Coast areas. It is very similar to the Olivaceous but characterised by its tail-flicking.

The **OLIVE-TREE WARBLER** (*Hippolais olivetorum*) is an uncommon passage migrant to Kuwait and has been reported very occasionally in the centre and in Asir. It is a little larger (6 inches) than other Hippolais warblers and is grey-brown all over with a paler throat and darker wings and tail. The bill is thicker and broader and the legs are dark grey.

The **BOOTED WARBLER** (*Hippolais caligata*) breeds occasionally in UAE and is an uncommon migrant in some eastern parts of the peninsula. Separated from other Hippolais by white outer tail feathers and its smaller size ($4\frac{1}{2}$ inches/11.4 cm).

**LEAF WARBLERS** *Phylloscopus.* Most members of this group are very small and they are characterised by short bills, flat foreheads and a habit of flicking their slightly forked tails. Many species within this group are extremely similar and can really only be separated by measuring wing formation.

Opposite above: *Scrub Warbler.*

## WILLOW WARBLER
*Phylloscupus trochilus*
## CHIFFCHAFF
*Phylloscopus collybita*
$4\frac{1}{4}$ inches (11cm)

*Identification:* Both species are darkish-grey-brown above with an eyestripe that varies from cream to pale yellow. The underparts are pale and also have varying degrees of yellow. Sometimes they can be separated by their legs which are generally paler in the Willow and dark grey or black in the Chiffchaff. Their song (seldom to be heard in this region) is an infallible guide – the Willow produces a musical series of descending notes whereas the Chiffchaff has just two notes 'Chiff chaff' repeated haphazardly. The Chiffchaff is generally found higher up in a tree than a Willow who is more likely to be in a low bush.

## SCRUB WARBLERS

The birds described below are actually from different groups but for convenience they are here being grouped together.

## SCRUB WARBLER
*Scotocerca inquieta*
4 inches (10cm)

*Identification:* This pretty, busy little bird, is sandy-grey above with faint darker streaks along its crown and mantle. The underparts are paler and variable in colour; in central Arabia they are mostly pale buffish-grey, whereas in Asir they have a distinct rosy tinge. The long tail is often cocked and flicked and the underside is faintly marked with grey and white. There is a black-tailed variety (illustrated on title page) found in one or two isolated wadis in the Riyadh area that is much greyer and streaked on the breast as well as on the upperparts and whose tail is totally black with no marking at all on the underside. The voice is a weak 'pee-wee, pee-wee' and 'teedle-wee'.

*Habitat:* Wadis and desert country with low bushes from which they dart to the ground and then quickly dart back again.

*Status in Central Arabia:* Resident breeding.

*Status in Arabian Peninsula:* Breeds in Eastern Province, Oman and UAE and probably also in Asir, Hejaz and the northwest.

*Habitat:* Trees and bushes.

*Status in Arabian Peninsula:* Willow – passage migrant. Chiffchaff – winter visitor.

Top right: *Black-tailed Scrub Warbler*.
Above: *Chiffchaff*. The Willow Warbler is illustrated on pages 132–3.

## GRACEFUL WARBLER
*Prinia gracilis*
4 inches (10cm)

*Identification:* This is another tiny little bird with a long tail which, as it darts from one bush to another, is rather reminiscent of a large and solid dragonfly. It is an untidy-looking bird which, when it pauses briefly on one twig before passing on to another one, seems not to have time to adjust its feathers properly. Consequently the slightly darker streaks on the warm brownish-grey upperparts are seldom

noticeable, though they are in fact there. The underside of the tail is quite strongly marked with black and a little white but the exact markings are hard to discern as the bird is never still. The voice is grating and seems improbably loud and ugly for such a small and pretty little bird.

*Habitat:* Anywhere where there are bushes and shrubs, particularly with water nearby.

*Status in Arabian Peninsula:* Resident breeding in most parts of the peninsula except for the centre and Kuwait.

## SYLVIA WARBLERS *Sylvia.*
These are characterised by slightly graduated tails which are rounded at the tip; they mostly have high foreheads, sometimes almost square-looking and there is often a ring round the eye.

138

Below left: *Graceful Warbler.*
Below: *The Whitethroat is a migrant from Europe.*

## WHITETHROAT
*Sylvia communis*
5½ inches (14cm)

*Identification:* The male has a grey head, the grey well below the eye and a white throat. The wings are darker grey, well-streaked with chestnut and the underparts are cream with a touch of pink on breast and flanks. There is a white circle round the eye, the legs are pale yellowish-brown and the outer tail feathers are white. The female is the same except that her head is brown rather than grey.

*Habitat:* Tamarisks bordering cultivation, gardens.

*Status in Central Arabia:* Passage migrant.

*Status in Arabian Peninsula:* Passage migrant in most areas.

## LESSER WHITETHROAT
*Sylvia curruca*
5¼ inches (13.5cm)

*Identification:* The crown, nape, mantle and tail are unstreaked grey; the grey wings have faint paler streaks; the cheeks are black and there is a white ring round the eye; the throat is white, underparts off-white and the outer tail feathers are white. The legs are dark grey. *S. c. minuta* which, until recently, was known as Lesser Desert Whitethroat, has a much less conspicuous cheek patch and is a more yellowish-grey on its upperparts.

*Habitat:* Gardens, palm groves and near cultivation.

*Status in Central Arabia:* Common passage migrant or winter visitor and a few birds have been observed in most months of the year.

## BARRED WARBLER
*Sylvia nisoria*
6 inches (15cm)

*Identification:* The Barred Warbler is one of the easiest warblers to identify. The very high and rounded head is dark grey as are the nape, mantle and tail. The wings have white tips to some of the feathers and the tips of the outer tail feathers are also white. The pale grey underparts have short crescent bars on the chin, throat, breast and flanks – these are also present on the rump and undertail coverts. The eye is bright yellow. The female is a browner grey, is less distinctly barred and the white at the tip of the outer tail feathers is almost non-existent.

*Habitat:* Acacia trees in gardens and at edges of cultivation.

*Status in Central Arabia:* Passage migrant.

*Status in Arabian Peninsula:* Passage migrant in Hejaz and Eastern Province.

Top left: *Male Barred Warbler.*
Left: *Female Barred Warbler.*

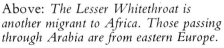

Above: *The Lesser Whitethroat is another migrant to Africa. Those passing through Arabia are from eastern Europe.*

*Status in Arabian Peninsula:* Winter visitor and passage migrant to most parts of the peninsula.

## GARDEN WARBLER
*Sylvia borin*
5½ inches (14cm)

*Identification:* Probably the best way to separate this warbler from other Sylvias is its total lack of distinguishing features. It is greyish-brown above with no eyestripe, wing bar or white outer tail feathers. It is pale yellowish-grey below without a white throat. The legs are grey, the very short bill is greyish-yellow and there is a faint ring round the eye.

*Habitat:* Palm groves and gardens.

*Status in Central Arabia:* Passage migrant.

*Status in Arabian Peninsula:* Uncommon passage migrant in Eastern Province.

Above: *Garden Warbler.*

## BLACKCAP
*Sylvia atricapilla*
$5\frac{1}{2}$ inches (14cm)

*Identification:* These birds are dark grey above and pale grey below with rufous on the flanks and undertail coverts. The male has a shallow black crown and the female a chestnut one. There is a distinct white *half*-circle below the eye.

*Habitat:* Bushes and tall scrub, generally in proximity to water.

*Status in Central Arabia:* Passage migrant

*Status in Arabian Peninsula:* Passage migrant to Hejaz, the northwest, Eastern Province and the Gulf Coast.

## DESERT WARBLER
*Sylvia nana*
$4\frac{1}{2}$ inches (11.5cm)

*Identification:* The Desert Warbler is a small sandy-coloured little bird with a pale chestnut tail and rump. The legs and bill vary from yellowish to quite a distinct orange. The eyes are yellow,

on some birds more markedly so than on others. There is a separate race of these birds (Siberian) which are also (less frequently) seen and which are very much greyer on the upperparts.

*Habitat:* Scrub desert, cultivated areas. Always found very close to the ground and often on the sand beside a low bush.

*Status in Central Arabia:* Common winter visitor.

*Status in Arabian Peninsula:* Winter visitor to most parts of the peninsula.

## ORPHEAN WARBLER
*Sylvia hortensis*
## ARABIAN WARBLER
*Sylvia leucomelaena*
6 inches (15cm)

*Identification:* There is much confusion in the separation of these two species which makes the sorting out of their individual status almost impossible at the present time. Both birds have black heads and black tails, are dark grey above and cream below. The Orphean has a less dense crown and white outer-tail feathers. The Arabian

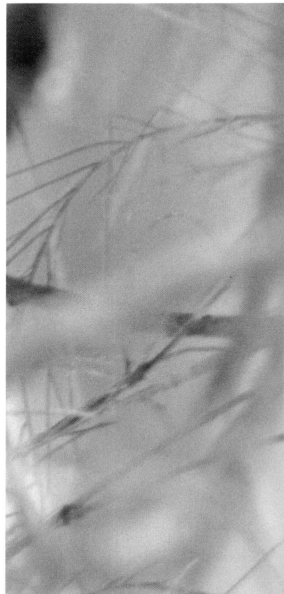

Top: *Male Blackcap.*

Above: *Desert Warbler.*

has a very distinct white ring round the eye and an almost completely black tail – the tips of the outer feathers are white but these are only noticeable on the underside when the bird is at rest. The Arabian's throat is a purer white than the Orphean's.

*Habitat:* Scrub desert with acacia, palm groves.

*Allied Specie*
**MENETRIES' WARBLER** (*Sylvia mystacea*) is a passage migrant and occasional winter visitor to most parts of the peninsula. It is dark grey above with a black crown extending well below the eye and a black tail edged with white. The underparts are off-white with pinkish-buff on throat and breast. The red eye is circled with pale yellow and the legs are flesh-coloured.

Below: *Orphean Warbler.*

## ABYSSINIAN WHITE-EYE
*Zosterops abyssinicus*
$4\frac{1}{2}$ inches (12cm)

*Identification:* This pretty, active little bird has a very conspicuous white eye-ring. The upperparts are dark olive-green; the throat and undertail coverts are pure, unstreaked, pale yellow and the rest of the underparts buffish. The song is an incessant soft 'tcheew, tcheew'.

*Habitat:* Tamarisk and flowering shrubs at high altitudes.

*Status in Arabian Peninsula:* Common resident in Asir.

## FLYCATCHERS
FLYCATCHERS *Muscicapidae.* This group of small birds feeds entirely on insects. They are usually perched on a prominent low branch of a tree or on a telegraph wire from which they make swift sorties after their prey and then generally return to the same perch. They have shortish, rather flattened bills.

## SPOTTED FLYCATCHER
*Muscicapa striata*
$5\frac{1}{2}$ inches (14cm)

*Identification:* This little bird has an unmistakable, almost vertical, posture and is always perched in a prominent place. The upperparts are dark brownish-grey with paler streaks on the wings and rows of dark spots on the slightly paler crown, running from the base of its bill to the top of the head. The underparts are off-white liberally streaked brown on throat and breast. Sexes are alike and juveniles are very spotted. At very close quarters a few black bristles can be seen at the base of the lower mandible.

*Habitat:* Palm groves and tamarisks bordering cultivation.

*Status in Central Arabia:* Passage migrant.

*Status in Arabian Peninsula:* Passage migrant to most parts of the peninsula.

*Allied Species*

The **SEMI-COLLARED FLYCATCHER** (*Ficedula semi-torquata*) is an uncommon passage migrant to most parts of the peninsula. The upperparts are black, the underparts white. There is a lot of white on the black wing, a white half collar and white on the forehead and outer tail feathers.

The **RED-BREASTED FLYCATCHER** (*Ficedula parva*) is an uncommon passage migrant to central and eastern parts of the peninsula. It is grey above, rufous on the throat and breast and cream on the rest of the underparts. The black tail has white on the basal outer-feathers.

The African **PARADISE FLYCATCHER** (*Terpsiphone viridis*) is seen in Asir. This startlingly beautiful bird has a deep turquoise head and neck, grey underparts with white at the undertail coverts. The wings and long rounded tail are rich chestnut, the male having very long tail streamers of the same colour.

Opposite: *The Abyssinian White-eye, as its name suggests, is one of the African birds that have extended their range north into Arabia.*

Above: *Spotted Flycatcher.*

**SUNBIRDS** *Nectariniidae.* These beautiful little birds are equivalent to the Hummingbirds of the Americas. Their long tubular tongues perform the same function for flowers as bees. Their bills are long and down-curved; they will catch small insects on the wing as well as taking the nectar from flowers.

### ORANGE-TUFTED SUNBIRD
*Nectarinia osea*
4–4½ inches (10–11 cm)

*Identification:* The male in breeding plumage (generally regained by October and retained until mid-summer) is irridescent purple on the crown and breast, bright electric blue on the throat, face, rump and base of upper tail, emerald green on the neck and mantle and is black on the belly and undertail. Out of about 30 birds observed at very close quarters only *one* had an orange tuft, and this was very clear from all angles. The females, which were outnumbered by their mates by about 15 to 1, are noticeably smaller than the males and are grey-brown above, paler below. As they fly overhead they utter a non-stop, abrupt 'Tck-tck-tck'. When moving around in a bush they emit a single-note whistle and a more grating and louder 'chirrk-chirrk'.

*Habitat:* Well-treed or cultivated wadis in mountain areas. In some wadis they are very plentiful and in others less so.

*Status in Arabian Peninsula:* Resident in Asir.

Top right: *Like the White-eye, these Sunbirds are representatives of the African bird-life. This is a female Orange Tufted Sunbird.*

Right: *Male Orange Tufted Sunbird.*

## INDIAN PURPLE SUNBIRD
*Nectarinia asiatica*
4–5 inches (10–12cm)

*Identification:* The male in full breeding plumage is an irridescent purple on its head, neck and throat, electric blue on the mantle and rump, dullish purple on the breast and belly and has black wings. In non-breeding plumage he is olive-brown above, dull yellow below with a broad black stripe, variable in width, running down his breast. During early autumn until mid-winter males can be seen looking patchy and untidy in various states of transitional plumage; at this time they may be purple above and quite a bright yellow below with blotches of black here and there. The female is like the non-breeding male but lacks the black band down her breast.

*Habitat:* Gardens, wooded areas, thorn trees among sand dunes.

*Status in Arabian Peninsula:* Resident breeding in UAE and Oman and in one or two places in Eastern Province.

*Allied Species*
The **SHINING SUNBIRD** (*Nectarinia habessinica*) has been observed in Asir. It is similar to Orange-Tufted but has more metallic green than blue plumage and has a dark scarlet band on the breast. The female is darkish brown all over.

The **PYGMY SUNBIRD** (*Anthreptes metallicus*) probably breeds in Asir. They have much shorter bills than the other sunbirds of the area and the breeding male is distinctive in having very long black central tail feathers. The entire front portion of his body is bright green and he has a yellow belly and black wings. Females and non-breeding males are brownish-grey above and yellowish below.

Above: *Female Indian Purple Sunbird.*

Left: *Indian Purple Sunbird.*

# Appendix 1

## Status and seasonal sightings of birds in central Arabia and in the Peninsula

* BREEDS
● COMMON
○ UNCOMMON

NW NORTHWESTERN SAUDI ARABIA
EP EASTERN PROVINCE OF SAUDI ARABIA
UAE UNITED ARAB EMIRATES

|  |  | *Central Arabia* | | | | | | | | | | | | *Arabian peninsula* |
|---|---|---|---|---|---|---|---|---|---|---|---|---|---|---|
|  |  | Jan | Feb | Mar | Apr | May | Jun | Jul | Aug | Sep | Oct | Nov | Dec |  |
| **1** |  |  |  |  |  |  |  |  |  |  |  |  |  |  |
| VULTURES | Egyptian★ | ● | ● | ● | ● | ● | ○ | ○ | ○ |  |  |  | ● | Hejaz, Asir, NW, EP UAE, Oman |
|  | Griffon★ | ○ | ○ | ○ | ○ | ○ |  | ○ |  | ○ | ○ | ○ | ○ | Hejaz, Asir, NW Oman, UAE |
|  | Black | ○ |  | ○ |  |  |  |  |  |  | ○ | ○ |  | NW UAE, Oman |
|  | Lappet-faced | ○ |  | ○ |  |  |  |  |  |  |  | ○ |  | Hejaz, NW UAE, Oman |
| EAGLES | Steppe | ● | ● | ● |  |  |  |  |  | ○ | ● | ● | ● | Hejaz, Asir, NW, EP Oman |
|  | Imperial | ○ | ○ |  |  |  |  |  |  |  | ○ | ○ |  | EP Oman |
|  | Lesser Spotted | ○ | ○ |  |  |  |  |  |  |  |  |  |  | EP Oman |
|  | Osprey |  |  | ○ | ○ |  |  |  |  | ○ | ○ |  |  | Hejaz★, NW, EP Oman★, UAE |
| BUZZARDS | Common |  |  |  |  |  |  | ○ |  | ○ | ○ |  |  | NW, EP |
|  | Long-legged★ | ○ | ○ | ○ | ○ | ○ |  | ○ | ○ | ○ |  | ○ |  | Hejaz, Asir, NW, EP Bahrain |
| KITE | Black |  | ○ | ○ |  |  |  |  |  | ○ |  |  |  | Hejaz★, NW, EP, Asir |
| HARRIERS | Marsh |  | ○ | ○ | ○ |  |  |  |  | ○ | ○ | ○ | ○ | Hejaz, NW UAE |
|  | Pallid |  |  | ○ | ○ |  |  | ○ |  | ○ | ○ |  |  | Hejaz, NW, EP UAE |
| HAWKS | Sparrowhawk | ○ | ○ |  |  |  |  |  |  | ○ | ○ | ○ |  | Hejaz, NW, EP, Asir |
| FALCONS | Barbary★ | ○ | ○ | ○ | ○ |  | ○ | ○ | ○ | ○ | ○ |  |  | Hejaz, Asir, NW, EP |
|  | Lanner★ | ○ |  | ○ |  |  |  |  |  |  |  |  |  | Hejaz, NW, EP★ |
|  | Kestrel★ | ○ | ○ | ○ | ○ | ○ | ○ |  | ○ | ○ | ○ | ○ | ○ | Hejaz, NW, EP, Asir UAE★, Oman, Bahrain |
|  | Lesser Kestrel★ | ○ | ○ | ○ |  |  |  |  |  | ○ | ○ | ○ | ○ | Hejaz, NW, EP, Asir |

Central Arabia — Arabian peninsula

| | | Jan | Feb | Mar | Apr | May | Jun | Jul | Aug | Sep | Oct | Nov | Dec | Arabian peninsula |
|---|---|---|---|---|---|---|---|---|---|---|---|---|---|---|
| OWLS | Little★ | ○ | ○ | | | | ○ | | ○ | | ○ | | ○ | Hejaz, Oman, UAE, Kuwait |
| | Hume's Tawny★ | ○ | | ○ | ○ | | | ○ | ○ | ○ | | | | Asir, NW |
| **2** | | | | | | | | | | | | | | |
| HERONS | Grey | | ○ | ○ | | ○ | | | | ○ | ○ | ○ | | Hejaz, Asir, NW, EP / Oman, Bahrain, UAE |
| | Purple | | | ○ | ○ | | | | ○ | ○ | ○ | ○ | ○ | Hejaz, NW, EP / Oman, Kuwait |
| | Squacco | | ○ | ○ | ● | ○ | ○ | ○ | ○ | ● | ○ | | | Hejaz, NW, EP / UAE, Oman, Bahrain |
| | Night | | ○ | | ○ | | | ○ | ○ | ○ | ○ | | | NW, EP |
| | Little Bittern | ○ | ○ | ○ | | ○ | ○ | ○ | ○ | ○ | ○ | ○ | | Gulf Coast |
| EGRETS | Great White | | | | ○ | | | | | ○ | | | | Hejaz, EP / Oman, Bahrain |
| | Little | | | ○ | ○ | ○ | | | ○ | ○ | ○ | ○ | | Hejaz, NW / Oman, Bahrain, UAE |
| | Yellow-billed | ○ | | | | | | | | | | ○ | | Hejaz / Bahrain |
| | Cattle | ○ | | ○ | ○ | | | ○ | ○ | ○ | | | | Hejaz, NW, EP / UAE |
| IBIS | Glossy | ○ | | ○ | | | | ○ | ○ | ○ | | | | Hejaz, Asir, NW, EP |
| CRAKE | Spotted | | | | ○ | ○ | | | ○ | ○ | ○ | ○ | ○ | EP |
| MOORHEN★ | | ○ | ○ | ○ | ○ | ○ | ○ | ○ | ○ | ○ | ○ | ○ | ○ | Asir, NW, EP / Bahrain, Oman |
| COOT | | ○ | ○ | ○ | ○ | ○ | ○ | | ○ | ○ | ○ | ○ | ○ | Asir, NW, EP / Bahrain, Oman |
| **3** | | | | | | | | | | | | | | |
| STILT | Black-winged | ○ | ○ | ○ | ○ | | ○ | ○ | ○ | ○ | ○ | ○ | ○ | Oman, UAE |
| PLOVERS | Ringed | | ○ | ● | ● | ○ | | | ○ | ○ | ● | ○ | ○ | Hejaz, NW, EP / Oman, UAE, Bahrain |
| | Little Ringed | ○ | ○ | ○ | ● | ● | ○ | | ○ | ● | ○ | ○ | | Hejaz, NW / Oman, UAE |
| | Kentish | ○ | ○ | ● | ● | ○ | | ○ | ○ | ● | ○ | ○ | | Hejaz, NW, EP / UAE, Oman, Bahrain |
| | Greater Sand | | | | | | ○ | ○ | ○ | | | | | Hejaz, NW, EP / Oman |
| | Turnstone | | | | | | | | ○ | ○ | ○ | | ○ | Hejaz, NW, EP / Bahrain, Oman, UAE |
| | Dunlin | | | ○ | ○ | ○ | ○ | | ○ | ○ | ○ | ○ | ○ | Hejaz, NW, EP / UAE, Oman, Bahrain |
| | Lapwing | ○ | ○ | | | | | | | | | ○ | ○ | NW, EP |
| STINTS | Little | ● | ● | ● | ● | ● | ● | ○ | ○ | ○ | ● | ● | ● | NW, EP / Oman, Bahrain |

|  |  | Central Arabia | | | | | | | | | | | | Arabian peninsula |
|---|---|---|---|---|---|---|---|---|---|---|---|---|---|---|
|  |  | Jan | Feb | Mar | Apr | May | Jun | Jul | Aug | Sep | Oct | Nov | Dec |  |
|  | Temminck's |  | ○ | ○ | ○ |  |  |  | ○ | ○ | ○ | ○ | ○ | NW, EP Oman |
|  | Knot |  |  |  |  |  |  |  |  | ○ |  |  |  | EP |
| SANDPIPERS | Broad-billed |  |  |  |  |  |  | ○ | ○ | ○ |  |  |  | EP Oman, Bahrain |
|  | Curlew |  |  |  | ○ | ○ | ○ | ○ | ○ | ○ | ○ | ○ | ○ | Hejaz, NW, EP UAE, Oman |
|  | Common | ○ |  | ○ | ○ | ○ | ○ | ○ | ○ | ○ | ○ | ○ | ○ | Hejaz, NW, EP UAE, Oman |
|  | Terek |  |  |  | ○ | ○ | ○ | ○ | ○ |  |  |  |  | Hejaz, EP UAE |
|  | Marsh | ○ | ○ | ○ |  |  |  |  | ○ | ○ | ○ |  | ○ | Hejaz, NW, EP |
|  | Wood | ○ | ○ | ○ | ● | ○ |  | ● | ● | ● | ○ | ○ | ○ | Hejaz, NW UAE, Oman |
|  | Green | ● | ● | ● | ● | ● | ○ | ○ | ○ | ● | ● | ● | ● | Hejaz, NW Oman |
|  | Greenshank |  | ○ | ○ | ○ | ○ | ○ | ○ | ○ | ○ | ○ | ○ | ○ | Hejaz, NW Oman, Bahrain |
|  | Redshank |  | ○ | ○ | ○ |  | ○ | ○ | ○ | ○ | ○ | ○ | ○ | NW, EP UAE, Oman, Bahrain |
|  | Spotted Redshank |  |  | ○ | ○ |  |  |  | ○ | ○ | ○ | ○ | ○ | NW, EP Oman |
|  | Ruff & Reeve | ○ | ○ | ○ | ○ | ● | ○ | ○ | ○ | ● | ● | ○ | ○ | Hejaz, NW, EP Oman |
| SNIPE |  | ● | ○ | ○ | ○ |  |  |  | ○ | ○ | ● | ● | ○ | NW, EP Oman, Bahrain |
| COURSER | Cream-coloured★ | ○ | ○ | ○ | ○ |  | ○ | ○ | ○ | ○ |  | ○ | ○ | EP Oman |
| PRATINCOLE | Collared |  |  |  | ○ | ○ | ○ | ○ | ○ | ○ | ○ |  |  | EP Oman |
| CURLEW | Stone |  |  |  |  | ○ |  |  |  | ○ | ○ |  |  | Hejaz, EP Oman |
| **4** DOVES | Rock★ | ○ | ○ | ○ | ○ | ○ | ○ | ○ | ○ | ○ | ○ | ○ | ○ | Hejaz, Asir, NW, EP UAE, Oman |
|  | Collared★ | ● | ● | ● | ● | ● | ● | ● | ● | ● | ● | ● | ● | NW, EP Oman, UAE, Bahrain |
|  | Turtle★ | ○ | ○ | ○ | ○ | ○ | ○ | ○ | ○ | ○ | ○ | ○ | ○ | Hejaz, NW, EP Oman |
|  | Namaqua★ |  |  | ○ | ○ | ○ | ○ | ○ | ○ | ○ | ○ |  |  | Hejaz, EP |
| **5** BEE-EATERS | Little Green★ | ● | ● | ● | ● | ● | ● | ● | ● | ● | ● | ● | ● | Hejaz, EP, NW UAE★, Oman |

| | | Central Arabia | | | | | | | | | | | | Arabian peninsula |
|---|---|---|---|---|---|---|---|---|---|---|---|---|---|---|
| | | Jan | Feb | Mar | Apr | May | Jun | Jul | Aug | Sep | Oct | Nov | Dec | |
| | European | | | ● | ● | ○ | | | ○ | ● | ● | ○ | | Hejaz, Asir, NW, EP / Oman |
| | Blue-cheeked | | ○ | ● | ○ | ○ | | | ○ | ○ | ● | ○ | | Hejaz, NW, EP / Oman |
| ROLLER | European | | | | ○ | ○ | ○ | | ○ | ○ | ○ | ○ | | Asir, NW, EP / Oman |
| HOOPOE★ | | | | ○ | ○ | ○ | ○ | ○ | ● | ● | ● | ○ | ○ | Hejaz, NW, EP / Oman, UAE |
| PARAKEET | Ring-necked | ○ | ○ | ○ | | | ○ | | | | | ○ | ○ | Hejaz, EP / Bahrain★, UAE★ |
| **6** | | | | | | | | | | | | | | |
| PARTRIDGE | Arabian Sand★ | ○ | ○ | ○ | ○ | ○ | ○ | ○ | ○ | ○ | ○ | ○ | | Hejaz, NW |
| WRYNECK | | | | ○ | ○ | ○ | | | ○ | ○ | | | | Hejaz, NW, EP |
| CUCKOO | | | | | ○ | | | | ○ | ○ | ○ | | ○ | Hejaz, NW, EP / Kuwait |
| SWIFTS | Common | | | ○ | ○ | ○ | ○ | ○ | | ○ | ○ | ○ | | Hejaz, NW, EP |
| | Pallid★ | | ○ | ○ | ○ | ○ | ○ | ○ | | | ○ | | ○ | Hejaz, NW / Oman |
| BULBUL | Yellow-vented★ | ● | ● | ● | ● | ● | ● | ● | ● | ● | ● | ● | ● | Hejaz, Asir, NW / Oman, UAE★ |
| BABBLER | Arabian★ | ○ | ○ | ○ | ○ | ○ | ○ | ○ | ○ | ○ | ○ | ○ | ○ | Hejaz, Asir / Oman, UAE★ |
| SWALLOWS | Common | ○ | ○ | ○ | ● | ● | ○ | ○ | ○ | ● | ● | ○ | ○ | Hejaz, NW, Asir, EP / Bahrain★, Oman, UAE |
| | Red-rumped | | | ○ | ○ | ○ | ○ | | ○ | ○ | ○ | | | Hejaz, Asir, EP |
| MARTINS | House | ○ | ○ | ○ | ○ | ○ | | | ○ | ○ | ○ | | | Hejaz, NW, EP |
| | Sand | ○ | ○ | ○ | ○ | ○ | ○ | ○ | ○ | ○ | ○ | ○ | ○ | Hejaz, NW, EP |
| | Pale Crag★ | ○ | ○ | ○ | ○ | ○ | ○ | ○ | ○ | ○ | ○ | ○ | ○ | Hejaz, NW, EP / Oman |
| | Crag | | | ○ | ○ | ○ | | | | | ○ | ○ | | Hejaz, NW, EP / UAE |
| **7** | | | | | | | | | | | | | | |
| RAVENS | Brown-necked★ | ● | ● | ● | ● | ● | ● | ● | ● | ● | ● | ● | ● | Hejaz, Asir, NW / Oman |
| | Fan-tailed★ | ○ | ○ | ○ | ○ | ○ | ○ | ○ | ○ | ○ | ○ | ○ | ○ | Hejaz, Asir, NW |
| STARLING | | ○ | ○ | ○ | | | | | ○ | ○ | ○ | | ○ | NW, EP / Oman, Bahrain |
| ORIOLES | Golden | | | ○ | ○ | ○ | ○ | | ○ | ○ | | | | Hejaz, NW, EP / Oman |
| | 'Gypsy' | | | ○ | | | | | | ○ | | | | Qasim |
| **8** | | | | | | | | | | | | | | |
| SHRIKES | Great Grey★ | ○ | ○ | ○ | ○ | ○ | ○ | ○ | ○ | ● | ● | ○ | ○ | Hejaz, Asir, NW, EP / Oman, UAE |

|  | | Central Arabia | | | | | | | | | | | | Arabian peninsula |
|---|---|---|---|---|---|---|---|---|---|---|---|---|---|---|
|  | | Jan | Feb | Mar | Apr | May | Jun | Jul | Aug | Sep | Oct | Nov | Dec | |
|  | Lesser Grey | ○ | ○ | ○ | ○ | ○ |  |  | ○ | ○ |  |  |  | Hejaz, NW, EP |
|  | Woodchat |  | ○ | ○ | ○ |  |  |  | ○ | ○ |  |  |  | Hejaz, NW, EP |
|  | Masked |  |  | ○ | ○ | ○ |  |  | ○ | ○ | ○ |  |  | Hejaz, NW, EP |
|  | Red-backed | ○ | ○ | ○ | ○ | ○ |  |  | ○ | ● | ○ | ○ | ○ | Hejaz, NW, EP |
|  | Isabelline | ○ | ○ | ○ | ○ | ○ |  |  | ○ | ○ | ○ | ○ | ○ | Hejaz, NW / Oman |
|  | 'Rufous' |  | ○ | ○ | ○ | ○ |  |  | ○ | ○ | ○ | ○ |  | Hejaz, NW, EP / Bahrain, UAE, Oman |
| HYPOCOLIUS | Grey | ○ | ○ | ○ | ○ |  |  |  |  | ○ |  | ○ | ○ | Hejaz★, EP |
| **9 WHEATEARS** | European | ○ | ○ | ○ | ○ | ○ | ○ |  |  | ○ |  |  |  | Hejaz, NW, EP / Bahrain, UAE, Oman |
|  | Desert | ○ | ○ | ○ | ○ |  |  |  | ○ | ○ | ○ |  | ○ | Hejaz, NW, EP / Oman, UAE |
|  | Isabelline | ○ | ● | ● | ○ | ○ |  | ○ | ○ | ○ | ● | ● | ○ | Hejaz, NW, EP / UAE, Oman |
|  | Black-eared | ○ | ○ | ○ | ○ |  |  |  | ○ | ○ | ○ |  | ○ | Hejaz, NW, EP / UAE, Oman |
|  | Mourning | ● | ● | ○ | ○ |  |  |  |  | ○ | ○ | ● | ● | Hejaz★, Asir★, NW, EP |
|  | Hume's |  |  | ○ |  |  |  |  |  |  | ○ |  |  | NW / Oman, UAE★ |
|  | Pied | ○ | ○ | ○ | ○ |  |  |  |  | ○ | ○ | ○ | ○ | Hejaz, Asir, NW, EP / UAE |
|  | Finsch's |  |  | ○ | ○ |  |  |  |  |  |  |  |  | NW / UAE |
|  | White-crowned Black★ | ○ | ○ | ○ | ○ | ○ | ○ | ○ | ○ | ○ | ○ | ○ | ○ | Hejaz, NW, EP★ / Kuwait |
|  | Hooded★ | ○ | ○ | ○ | ○ | ○ | ○ | ○ | ○ | ○ | ○ |  |  | Hejaz, EP |
|  | Red-tailed | ○ | ○ | ○ |  |  |  |  | ○ | ○ | ○ |  |  | NW, EP / Oman |
| **10 THRUSHES** | Song |  | ○ | ○ | ○ | ○ |  |  |  |  |  | ○ | ○ | Asir, Hejaz, EP / Bahrain |
|  | Black-throated |  |  |  |  |  |  |  |  |  | ○ |  | ○ | EP |
|  | Rock |  | ○ | ○ | ○ |  |  |  |  |  |  |  |  | Hejaz, Asir, EP / Oman |
|  | Blue Rock | ○ | ○ | ○ | ○ |  |  |  |  | ○ | ○ |  | ○ | Hejaz, Asir, NW, EP / Oman |
| **BLACKSTART★** | | ○ | ● | ● | ● | ● | ● | ○ | ○ | ○ | ○ | ○ | ○ | Hejaz, Asir, NW |

| | | | | Central Arabia | | | | | | | | | Arabian peninsula |
|---|---|---|---|---|---|---|---|---|---|---|---|---|---|
| | | Jan | Feb | Mar | Apr | May | Jun | Jul | Aug | Sep | Oct | Nov | Dec | |
| REDSTARTS | Common | | | ○ | ○ | ○ | | ○ | | ○ | ○ | ○ | | Hejaz, Asir, NW, EP / UAE |
| | Black | | ○ | ○ | ○ | | | | | ○ | ○ | ○ | ○ | Hejaz, Asir, NW, EP / Oman, UAE |
| NIGHTINGALES | | | | ○ | ○ | ○ | | | | ○ | ○ | | | EP |
| | Thrush- | | | | ○ | ○ | | | ○ | ○ | | | | Hejaz, EP |
| BLUETHROAT | | ○ | ○ | ○ | ○ | | | | ○ | ○ | ○ | ○ | ○ | Hejaz, NW, EP / Oman |
| BUSH CHATS | Black★ | | ○ | ○ | ○ | ○ | ○ | ○ | ○ | ○ | ○ | | | Hejaz |
| | Rufous★ | | ○ | ○ | ● | ● | ○ | ○ | ○ | ○ | ○ | | | Hejaz, NW, EP / Oman |
| ROBIN | White-throated | | | ○ | ○ | | | | ○ | | | ○ | | Hejaz, EP |
| STONECHAT | | ○ | ○ | ○ | ○ | | | ○ | ○ | ○ | ○ | ○ | ○ | Hejaz, Asir, NW, EP |
| WHINCHAT | | | | ○ | ○ | | | | ○ | ○ | | | | Hejaz, NW, EP |
| **II** | | | | | | | | | | | | | | |
| PIPITS | Tawny | ○ | ○ | ○ | ○ | ○ | | | ○ | ○ | ● | ● | ○ | Hejaz, NW, EP / Oman |
| | Tree | | | ○ | ○ | ○ | | | | ○ | ○ | | | Hejaz, NW, EP / UAE |
| | Red-throated | | | ○ | ○ | ○ | | | | ○ | ○ | ○ | | Hejaz, NW, EP |
| | Water/Rock | ○ | ○ | ○ | ○ | | | | | ○ | ○ | | ○ | NW / Oman, UAE, Bahrain |
| WAGTAILS | White | ● | ● | ● | ● | | ○ | | | ○ | ● | ● | ● | Hejaz, Asir, NW, EP / Bahrain, Oman, UAE |
| | Grey | | ○ | ○ | ○ | | | | ○ | ○ | ○ | ○ | | Asir, NW, EP / Oman, Bahrain |
| | Yellow | ○ | ○ | ○ | ○ | ○ | ○ | ○ | ○ | ○ | ○ | ○ | ○ | Hejaz, NW, EP / UAE |
| **I2** | | | | | | | | | | | | | | |
| LARKS | Hoopoe★ | ○ | ○ | ● | ○ | ○ | ○ | ○ | ○ | ○ | ○ | ○ | ○ | Hejaz, NW, EP★ / Oman |
| | Black-crowned Finch★ | | ○ | ○ | ○ | ○ | ○ | ○ | ○ | ○ | ○ | | | Hejaz, EP★ / Oman, UAE |
| | Lesser Short-toed★ | ○ | ○ | ○ | ○ | ○ | | ○ | ○ | ○ | ○ | | ○ | Hejaz, NW, EP / Oman |
| | Short-toed | ○ | ○ | ○ | ○ | | | | ○ | ○ | ○ | | ○ | Hejaz, NW, EP |
| | Temminck's Horned★ | ○ | ○ | ○ | ○ | | | | | | ○ | | ○ | NW / Kuwait★ |
| | Crested★ | ● | ● | ● | ● | ● | ● | ● | ● | ● | ● | ● | ● | Throughout |
| | Desert★ | ● | ● | ● | ● | ● | ● | ● | ● | ● | ● | ● | ● | Hejaz, NW, EP★ |

| | | Jan | Feb | Mar | Apr | May | Jun | Jul | Aug | Sep | Oct | Nov | Dec | Arabian peninsula |
|---|---|---|---|---|---|---|---|---|---|---|---|---|---|---|
| | | | | | | _Central Arabia_ | | | | | | | | |
| | Bar-tailed★ | ● | ● | ● | ● | ● | ○ | ○ | ○ | ○ | ● | ● | ● | Hejaz, NW, EP★ |
| | Dunn's★ | ○ | ○ | ○ | ○ | ○ | ○ | ○ | ○ | ○ | ○ | ○ | ○ | Hejaz, NW, EP★ |
| **13** FINCH | Trumpeter★ | ○ | ○ | ○ | ○ | ○ | ○ | ○ | ○ | ○ | ○ | ○ | ○ | Hejaz, NW, EP★ |
| SPARROWS | House★ | ● | ● | ● | ● | ● | ● | ● | ● | ● | ● | ● | ● | Throughout |
| | Pale Rock | | | ○ | ○ | ○ | ○ | ○ | ○ | ○ | | | | EP |
| BUNTINGS | House★ | ○ | ○ | ○ | ○ | ○ | ○ | ○ | ○ | ○ | ○ | ○ | ○ | Hejaz, EP, Asir UAE★ |
| | Ortolan | | | | ○ | ○ | | | ○ | ○ | ○ | | | Hejaz, NW, EP UAE |
| **14** WARBLERS | Reed | | | ○ | ○ | ○ | | | ○ | ○ | ○ | ○ | | NW, EP Oman, Bahrain |
| | Great Reed | | | ○ | ○ | ○ | | | ○ | ○ | ○ | ○ | | NW Oman, Bahrain |
| | Clamorous | | | | | | | ○ | ○ | ○ | | | | Oman |
| | Sedge | | ○ | ○ | ○ | ○ | ○ | | | ○ | ○ | | | Hejaz, NW, EP |
| | Olivaceous★ | | | ○ | ○ | ○ | | | ○ | ○ | ○ | | | NW EP |
| | Icterine | | | | | | | | ○ | ○ | ○ | | | EP |
| | Chiffchaff | ○ | ○ | ○ | ○ | ○ | | | | ○ | ○ | ○ | | Hejaz, NW, EP UAE, Bahrain |
| | Willow | | | | ○ | ○ | ○ | | ○ | ○ | ○ | | | Hejaz, NW, EP UAE |
| | Scrub★ | ○ | ○ | ○ | ○ | ○ | ○ | ○ | ○ | ○ | ○ | ○ | ○ | Hejaz, Asir, NW, EP Oman, UAE★ |
| | Whitethroat | | ○ | | ○ | ○ | | | ○ | ○ | ○ | | | Hejaz, NW, EP |
| | Lesser Whitethroat | ○ | ○ | ○ | ○ | ○ | ○ | | ○ | ○ | ○ | ○ | ○ | Hejaz, NW, EP Oman |
| | Garden | | | | ○ | ○ | | | ○ | ○ | ○ | | | EP |
| | Barred | | | | ○ | ○ | ○ | | ○ | ○ | ○ | | | Hejaz, EP |
| | Blackcap | | ○ | ○ | ○ | ○ | | | | ○ | ○ | ○ | | Hejaz, Asir, NW, EP Bahrain |
| | Desert | ● | ● | | | | | | | ○ | ● | ● | ● | Hejaz, NW, EP Oman |
| FLYCATCHERS | Spotted | | | ○ | ○ | ○ | ○ | | ○ | ○ | ○ | ○ | | Throughout |
| | Semi-collared | | ○ | ○ | ○ | ○ | | | | | | | | Gulf Coast |

# Appendix 2

## *The Riyadh area*

Riyadh lies on the Wadi Hanifah which collects much of the drainage from the eastern slopes of the Tuwaiq escarpment to the northwest. Its average elevation is about 700 metres.

West of the town the land rises gently to the crest of the escarpment at which point it changes direction; the faulting here has produced a complex system of rocky wadis. The escarpment itself (in both directions) and the high rocky cliffs bordering Wadis Awsat and Nisah provide mountainous terrain quite near the capital. Beyond are belts of sand.

To the northeast there is another belt of sand (Irq Banban) with a second, smaller escarpment (Jebel Buwaib) beyond. This area contains relatively little cultivation but some of the small wadis on the back of the Buwaib escarpment accumulate water after rain and can quickly be transformed with quite lush vegetation. This is particularly so beyond Towqi. Further east still, some 100 kilometres from Riyadh, beyond a large tract of stony desert, the extensive Dahna sands are to be found.

Travelling north from Riyadh, towards Majma'ah, access can be obtained to the Wadi Hanifah and its tributaries. A left turn off the road past the Palaces, at almost any point, will lead to one of the many villages with palm groves and cultivated areas. Higher up, the wadis are drier and broader with acacia and other scrub.

Southeast of Riyadh the Wadi Hanifah, together with several other wadis cutting through the Tuwaiq escarpment at its bend, drains towards Al Kharj. This lies in a large hollow in which the water table is relatively high and cultivation over an extensive area is possible.

South of Riyadh, around Mansouriyah on the Ha'ir road, the drainage from the city has, in recent years, produced permanent water over

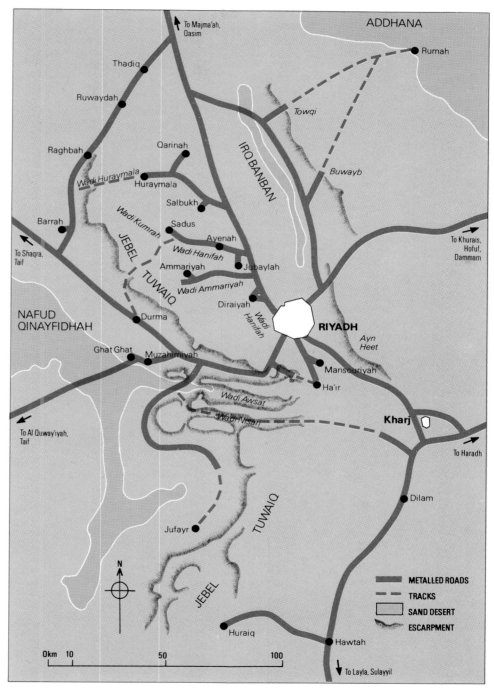

an extensive section of the Wadi Hanifah, with quite sizeable lakes surrounded by rushes, tamarisk and other shrubs.

# Appendix 3

*Birds found in the Arabian Peninsula but not in central Arabia except, in a few cases, as vagrants*

\* BREEDS       EP EASTERN PROVINCE OF SAUDI ARABIA
NW NORTHWESTERN SAUDI ARABIA       UAE UNITED ARAB EMIRATES

| | | *Asir* | *Oman* | *Gulf Coast* | *Elsewhere* |
|---|---|:---:|:---:|:---:|---|
| **1** | | | | | |
| VULTURE | Lammergeier | ●★ | | ● | Hejaz (Taif), NW |
| EAGLES | White-tailed | | ● | ● | |
| | Booted | ● | | ● | |
| | Bonelli's | ● | | ● | |
| BUZZARD | Honey | ● | | | |
| HAWKS | Goshawk | ● | | ● | |
| | Chanting Goshawk | ● | | | |
| FALCONS | Peregrine | | | ● | Hejaz |
| | Saker | | | ● | NW |
| | Hobby | | | ● | NW |
| OWLS | Scops | | | ●★ | Hejaz |
| | Eagle | | | ●★(EP) | NW |
| | Barn | | | ●★ | Hejaz |
| **2** | | | | | |
| HERONS | Goliath | | | | Hejaz, NW |
| | Reef | | ● | ● | Hejaz |
| | Bittern | | ● | ● | |
| SPOONBILL | | | ● | ● | Hejaz |
| HAMERKOP | | ● | | | Hejaz |
| STORKS | White | | | ● | Hejaz |
| | Black | | | ● | |
| **3** | | | | | |
| PLOVERS | Crab | ● | ● | ●★(Kuwait) | Hejaz |
| | Lesser Sand | | ● | ● | |
| | Golden | | ● | ● | |
| | Grey | | ● | ● | Hejaz, NW |
| | Red-wattled Lapwing | | ●★ | ●★(UAE) | |

| | | Asir | Oman | Gulf Coast | Elsewhere |
|---|---|---|---|---|---|
| | White-tailed Lapwing | | ● | | |
| | Sanderling | | ● | ● | Hejaz |
| SANDPIPER | Broad-billed | | ● | ● | |
| GODWITS | Bar-tailed | | ● | ● | Hejaz |
| | Black-tailed | | ● | ● | |
| CURLEW | Common | | ● | ● | Hejaz |
| | Slender-billed | | ● | ● | |
| WHIMBREL | | | ● | ● | |
| **4** | | | | | |
| DOVES & PIGEONS | Palm/Laughing | ● | ● | ●★(UAE) | NW |
| | Pink-breasted | ● | | | |
| | Red-eyed | ● | | | |
| | Bruce's Green | ● | ● | | Hejaz (Taif) |
| **5** | | | | | |
| KINGFISHERS | European | ● | ● | ●★(Bahrain) | NW |
| | Pied | | | ● | |
| | Grey-headed | ● | | | |
| BEE-EATER | White-throated | | | | Hejaz |
| ROLLERS | Indian | | ●★ | ●★(UAE) | |
| | Abyssinian | ● | | | |
| HORNBILL | Grey | ● | | | |
| **6** | | | | | |
| WOODPECKER | Arabian | ● | | | Hejaz (Taif) |
| QUAIL | | ●★ | | | |
| FRANCOLIN | Grey | | ●★ | ●★(UAE) | |
| GUINEAFOWL | Tufted | ●★ | | | |
| CUCKOO | Great Spotted | ● | | ● | |
| SWIFTS | Alpine | ● | | ● | Hejaz |
| | Little | | | ● | |
| BULBUL | White-eared | | | ●★ | |
| **7** | | | | | |
| RAVEN | European | ● | | | |
| CROW | Indian House | | ●★ | ● | Hejaz |
| MAGPIE | European | ● | | | |
| STARLINGS | Violet-backed | ● | | | Hejaz |
| | Rose-coloured | | | ● | |
| GRACKLE | Tristram's | ●★ | | | Hejaz (Taif) |

|  |  | Asir | Oman | Gulf Coast | Elsewhere |
|---|---|---|---|---|---|
| **9** WHEATEARS | Red-breasted | ● | | | |
| | Red-rumped | | | ● | |
| **10** THRUSH | Yemen | ● | | | |
| **11** WAGTAIL | Citrine | | | ● | Hejaz, NW |
| **13** FINCHES | Chaffinch | | | ● | |
| | Gold | | | ● | NW |
| | Green | | | | NW |
| | Desert | | | | NW |
| | Sinai Rose– | | | | NW |
| LINNET | Yemen | ● | | | |
| SPARROWS | Arabian Golden | ● | | ●(Kuwait) | |
| | Yellow-throated | | ● | ●★(UAE) | |
| WEAVER | Ruppell's | ●★ | | | Hejaz★ |
| SILVERBILL | | ● | ● | ●★(UAE) | |
| BUNTING | Reed | | | ● | |
| **14** WARBLERS | Moustached | | | ●★(EP) | NW |
| | Booted | | | ●★(UAE) | |
| | Olive-tree | | | ●(Kuwait) | |
| | Graceful | ● | ● | ●★(EP) | Hejaz |
| WHITE-EYE | Abyssinian | ● | | | |
| FLYCATCHERS | Red-breasted | | | ● | |
| | African Paradise | ● | | | |
| SUNBIRDS | Orange-tufted | ●★ | | | Hejaz |
| | Indian Purple | | ●★ | ●★(UAE) | |
| | Shining | ● | | | |
| | Pygmy | ● | | | |

# References

**Ali, Salim.** *The Book of Indian Birds.* Diocesan Press, Bombay, 1955

**Benson, S. Vere.** *Birds of Lebanon and the Jordan Area.* International Council for Bird Preservation, 1970

**Heinzel, Fitter and Parslow.** *The Birds of Britain and Europe, with North Africa and the Middle East.* Collins, London, 1972

**Honeywell, R. A. and G. E.** *Birds of Batinah of Oman.* Ebenezer Baylis Limited, England, 1976

**Hutchinson, M.** 'Systematic List of Birds observed at or near Riyadh'. *Journal of the Saudi Arabian Natural History Society*, Number 14, 1975

**King, B. F.** 'April Birds Observations in Saudi Arabia'. *Journal of the Saudi Arabian Natural History Society*, Number 21, 1976

**Meinertzhagen, R.** *Birds of Arabia.* Oliver and Boyd, Edinburgh, 1954

**Peterson, Mountfort and Hollom.** *A Field Guide to the Birds of Britain and Europe.* Collins, London 1974

**Porter, Willis, Christensen and Neilsen.** *Flight Identification of European Raptors.* T. and A. D. Poyser, 1978

**Prozesky, O. P. M.** *A Field Guide to the Birds of Southern Africa.* Collins, London, 1974

*'The Emirates'.* Number 24, November 1978

*The Ornithological Society of the Middle East Bulletin.* Numbers 1, 2 and 3

**Williams, J. G.** *A Field Guide to the Birds of East and Central Africa.* Collins, London, 1972

# Index

*References to appendices are in italics*